Street Women and the Art of Bullshitting

Street Women and the Art of Bullshitting
© Monique Layton 2010
ISBN   978-1-926820-20-0

Photographs in text © courtesy of Lincoln Clarkes (Worldwide Green Eyes)
Cover photograph © by Nick Didlick courtesy Vancouver *Sun*
Photograph Layton and Levi-Strauss © courtesy Simon Davies

Printing and Retailing for this publication outsourced to Lulu Books. Wholesaling
by Ingram Books.

Webzines of Vancouver
2901-969 Richards Street Vancouver BC Canada V6B 1A8
1.604.739.8130 webzines@anthropologising.ca
www.anthropologising.ca/webzines/webzines

Monique Layton with Claude Levi-Strauss during his visit to the University of
British Columbia in 1974.
© courtesy Simon Davies

Street Women and the Art of Bullshitting

The Oral Culture of Female Prostitutes and Drug Addicts in Vancouver

Monique Layton

Webzines
Vancouver 2010

NOTE

The research for this book was done during the 1970s and led to a report to the B.C. Police Commission in 1975, "Prostitution in Vancouver (1973-1975). Formal and Informal Reports"; to a doctoral dissertation, "Street Women and Their Verbal Transactions. Aspects of the Oral Culture of Female Prostitute Drug Addicts" (University of British Columbia, 1978); and to an article, "The Ambiguities of the Law: The Streetwalker's Dilemma." *Chitty's Law Journal* 27:109-120 (1979).

Vancouver, 2010.

Table of Contents

Chapter One

FRAME OF REFERENCE: LITERATURE **AND THEORY**

Prostitutes claim to have developed a quick appreciation of men as potential customers and the ability to manage them. Prostitutes who solicit in public places and who are also drug addicts explain that their twice vulnerable position with regard to the law increases their need for effectiveness. They claim to seek only quick financial rewards and to feel no compunction in shortchanging those they believe to be out to exploit them.

The social and legal vulnerability which results from their visible and illegitimate activities also leads them to seek acceptance into a supportive milieu where they find understanding and solidarity. At the same time, they stress the value of being self-sufficient and knowledgeable enough not to be "ripped off" by other street addicts. From the beginning, they must quickly learn the rules of behaviour that will enable them to cope with an ambivalent milieu, rules through which they will earn and retain acceptance into the subculture.

This study describes two types of verbal transactions practised by female prostitutes and drug addicts on the street: Those aimed at outsiders through what they describe as *conning,* and those that serve to socialize insiders through the use of didactic gossip. Both forms are loosely described by the informants as *bullshitting,* a technique of verbal exchange with which they appear to support both deceptive and cohesive transactions.

An understanding of the informants' verbal performances must rest on an understanding of their cultural values, and this study attempts to describe how they perceive and construct their socio-economic environment and how they interact within it. The addict-prostitutes studied here are thus described in terms of their subculture's worldview and their understanding of the conflicts between their system of cultural values and that of the larger society.

LITERATURE AND ETHNOSEMANTIC APPROACHES

A comprehensive bibliography of all the fictional, psychological, medical, legal, historical, sociological, and anthropological works devoted to the topic of the woman who makes her living on the street—even without considering the fast growing list of works related to the lifestyle of drug addicts and the problems of drug addiction—would be difficult to compile. Moreover, much of what has been written on the subject would not be relevant to the type of analysis and the point of view adopted here. If we look at the psychological, sociological, and anthropological literature related to prostitutes and prostitution, we find that the trend, until very recently, has been to consider the topic in terms of "morality, maladjustment, and rehabilitation" (James 1972a:8). Of those works, the best known are perhaps Benjamin and Master's *Prostitution and Morality* (1964), which develops the theme of the failure of rehabilitation as it is now attempted; and Mary Choisy's *Psychoanalysis of the Prostitute* (1965) and Harold Greenwald's *The Elegant Prostitute* (1970), which both offer a psychiatric approach to the study of call girls. Most of these works focus on the views of the larger society as it contemplates what it understands to be the world of the prostitute.

In contrast to those works devoted to the prostitutes' personality structure or to the social problems presented by what is deemed to be a morally reprehensible and physically detrimental lifestyle, a few studies concentrate on the women's (since only female prostitutes are considered here) own perspective and understanding of the environment in which they operate. Hirschi's "The Professional Prostitute" (1962) examines prostitution as an occupation and briefly attempts to give an insight into the practitioner's occupational ideology; Jackman, O'Toole, and Geis (1968) are concerned with the prostitute's self-image, and Velarde (1975), in "Becoming Prostitutes," with the way a masseuse-prostitute forms her self-identity; finally James's doctoral dissertation (1972a) offers an ethnosemantic approach to the study of streetwalkers. The latter work, with its taxonomic and componential analysis of the domains of the streetwalkers' argot, is (to my knowledge) the first study of its kind to concentrate exclusively on these informants' perception of their environment.[1]

Studies of drug addicts and drug addiction follow a parallel line, although in this case the social problems perceived are of a more recent nature. Agar, in contrast with previous works dealing mainly with the problem of the social and psychological "failure system" of the addict, present in *Ripping and Running* (1973) a similar approach to James's in her study of streetwalkers. Before him, Sutter's description of the world of the "righteous dope fiend" (1966) provides a good introduction to the subculture of the street addict. As well, Preble and Casey's ethnography of the heroin user's life on the street, "Taking Care of Business" (1969), seeks to find the meaning of *the life* for the street addict. In his survey of the literature of drug addiction. Weppner notes that Preble's anthropological field work, which resulted in that article (the first one emically oriented to deal with the user's life on the street,) was the impetus for other anthropologists "to study the street addict's subculture from his point of view and not from the abstracted empirical viewpoint of the sociologist or psychologist" (Weppner 1973:114). Finally, Stoddart's study (1968) should be mentioned, of particular interest here since some of his data on drug transactions are drawn from the same city ten years earlier and provides a useful source of comparison with data obtained for our study.

Both James and Agar's studies take an ethnosemantic approach. In *Ripping and Running,* Agar, who was mostly involved in institutional

---

[1] Schultz' definition of environment is adopted here: that part of the external world that can be directly apprehended. "This would include not only the physical but also the social environment with all of its natural artifacts, language, etc." (1967:170)

research, adapts a technique for gathering retrospective data to the definition of what he sees as conflict situations: his informants were asked to enact street scenes familiar to all addicts (e.g. obtaining money for drugs through various means, buying and using drugs); these enactments were tape recorded and later played back to other informants for validity and reliability checks. Both he and James borrow from linguistic methods and adopt in their work a systematic questioning procedure to elicit data which enable them to analyze the culture under study. In the componential analysis procedure they follow, the initial step is to provide the informants with "substitution frames" through which the ethnographers generate terminological systems. Next, they establish taxonomies by grouping "segregates" and "contrast sets" (Frake 1972; Psathas 1972:209; Agar 1973:28-39). The added sum of folk taxonomies thus obtained constitutes "a society's ethnoscience, its particular ways of classifying its material and social universe": in other words, it constitutes its "culture." (Sturtevant 1964:99) In a later work, *Ethnography and Cognition* (1974), Agar further expands on the methodology of "retrieving both concepts and their relationships" by examining "signs" in informants' utterances (1974:13). Folk taxonomies, already the subject of much of James's work, are examined again by Agar in this 1974 work as a means of investigating the informants' conceptualization of their environment.

Applying the same ethnoscientific approach as Agar and James, Spradley makes a formal semantic analysis of tramps and alcoholics in "Adaptive Strategies of Urban Nomads" (1972) and *You Owe Yourself a Drunk* (1970) and, with Mann, to a female occupation in an essentially male world in *The Cocktail Waitress* (1975). Because of their ethnosemantic approach, Agar, James, and Spradley break away from the conventional analysis of such subcultures as that of the heroin addict, the streetwalker, or the alcoholic, as *deviant* cultures; they define instead the way their informants perceive and order their environment and explain their actions in terms of these perceptions.

The repudiation of classical grammar by linguistic analysis and its description of each language in terms appropriate to its own structure have to a certain extent guided cultural anthropology along the same path. Thus, cognitive anthropology focuses on relationships between units of language and units of cognition and has travelled from an essentially *etic* viewpoint to an essentially *emic* understanding.

Conventionally, Pike's emic-etic distinction is used here for the description of behaviour, where etics mean features assumed to be culture-free, to which are compared emics, or the group's culture-bound apprehension of these same features. Harris's definitions were found the most useful guidelines for the usage of the two terms:

> Emic statements refer to logico-empirical systems whose phenomenal distinctions or "things" are built up out of contrasts and discriminations significant, meaningful, real, accurate, or in some other fashion regarded as appropriate by the actors themselves. An emic statement can be falsified if it can be shown that it contradicts the cognitive calculus by which relevant actors judge that entities are similar or different, real, meaningful, significant, or in some other sense "appropriate" or "acceptable." (Harris 1968:671)

By comparison with these statements which reflect exclusively the point of view of members of the subculture and ascertain their cultural competence,

> Etic statements depend upon phenomenal distinctions judged appropriate by the community of scientific observers. Etic statements cannot be falsified if they do not conform to the actor's notion of what is significant, real, meaningful or appropriate. Etic statements are verified when independent observers using similar operations agree that a given event has occurred (Harris 1968: 675).

I have adopted the emic perspective throughout this work and have tried to examine street women's perception of material phenomena and their cognitive discriminations. As in the works of Agar, Spradley, and

James, in which folk taxonomies reveal the culture's cognitive structure, the starting point of my fieldwork was the elaboration of linguistic categories and folk taxonomies for what the informants recognize as distinct domains.

I have tried to described the informants' apprehension of the socio-economic environment in which their practice their verbal transactions in two ways. I used both the cognitive constructs revealed by the taxonomy with the added dimension of folklore and verbal performances that call for "some dramatization of the ideals of the group" (Abrahams 1970:290), and the elicitation of stereotyped definitions that justify and reinforce the acknowledged confrontation between the subculture and larger culture.

FOLKLORE

Since folklorists view folklore as "raw material for the study of human thought" (Dundes1971:103), the study of a people's folklore may be taken as an intrinsic part of cognitive anthropology. Adopting Abrahams' (1971:17) definition of folklore as "all traditional expressions and implementations of knowledge operating within a community," knowledge is considered to be "the power of the mind for solving problems" and traditional knowledge to provide "inherited solutions to the recurrent problems of groups."

Some recurrent problems may be solved by material and practical means and the development of specific techniques. For instance, in the addict prostitute's culture, items of material folklore deal with the practical problems of fixing, transporting illegal drugs, tattooing, shoplifting, sexual practices, etc. Other problems, of an ethical or social order, find traditional solutions in ethical and aesthetic expression, often in the form of proverbs that provide "an argument for a course of action which conforms to community values" and "invokes an aura of moral rightness in the conversation. (Abrahams 1968:150)

As a communicative process, folklore is limited to relatively small groups, whose members (performers and audience) are part of the same reference group. Whatever the form of exchange and the folkloric genre used (tale, proverb, joke), it is transcended by the expression of notions that Dundes (1971:95) calls "folk ideas": the "traditional notions that a group of people have about the nature of man, of the world, and of man's life in the world." All cultures have underlying assumptions and it is their assumptions that:

> Folk ideas… are the building blocks of worldviews. Any one worldview will be based upon many individual folk ideas which contribute to the formation of that worldview. (Dundes 1971:96)

One of the folk ideas emerging from a corpus of proverbs and traditional phrases, for instance, would appear to be in North American culture the "principle of unlimited good" (in direct opposition to the "principle of limited good" found by Foster (1967) to be a characteristic notion in Mexican and other peasant cultures). This principle emerges ambiguously in my informants' belief that *marks* are plentiful and in the carelessness of some of their transactions since they assume that new opportunities will always arise. On the other hand, the pressure exercised by their needs as heroin addicts often make their soliciting a competitive enterprise. But it is also a fact that in that particular case, "good" (i.e. tricks) is indeed a limited commodity and one's gain is someone else's loss.

Dundes opposed "folk fallacies" to folk ideas and attributes the term to traditional stereotypes. As part of the "stated premises of a culture," they are contrasted to folk ideas of which one may not be aware or which one may not be able to articulate.

> Folk ideas would be more a matter of basic unquestioned premises concerning the nature of man, of society, and of the world, and these premises although manifested in folklore proper might not be all obvious to the folk in whose thinking they are

> central. Folk fallacies such as stereotypes would
> therefore be part of the conscious or self-conscious
> culture of a people whereas folk ideas would be part
> of the unconscious or, unself-conscious culture of a
> people. (Dundes 1971:101)

Street people interact in a close and active symbiosis with straight people who they see as trying to use, control, trap, exploit, and imprison them, and whom they try to evade, con, manipulate, rob, trick, and seduce. Much of their folklore, especially in the form of gossip and anecdotes, describes how this interaction takes place and how people deal with what they perceive to be a problem created by the conflict of interests between the two groups. To that extent, it reveals the precepts and norms of the informants' cognitive system. Gossip may also be seen as a means of achieving social control. It makes "a statement of approval or condemnation which reiterates the approved behavioural limits of the group." (Abrahams 1970:100)

If is true that folklore lives by force of its function, as folklorists often maintain, then it is the function of street folklore that we must examine. We often see it protecting its practitioners. For instance, the function of one of the well-typified villains (the *rat)* is clearly to shoulder and bear the responsibility for the informants' lack of competence. Much like scapegoats, they are depicted as loathsome and despicable so they can serve a useful function in enabling informants to refute or deny what would otherwise be seen as their own failures.

The conscious statements made by stereotypes strengthen the boundaries between the two groups, affirming a much-needed insiders' solidarity and defining the means of coping with outsiders; these often form the topic of gossip and anecdotes.

Jokes are also used as a protective device and allow apparently threatening behaviour to be perceived as a tentative or harmless incursion into otherwise forbidden areas. Their symmetrical or asymmetrical exchange (depending on people's individual prestige, their *reputation* or their *name) is* typically such "that in any other social context it would express and arouse hostility." (Radcliffe-Brown 1952:91) Since one of the functions of joking relationships is to obviate quarrels or real conflicts, it is not surprising that, just as they are found among cocktail waitresses (Spradley and Mann 1975) or longshoremen (Filcher 1972), they should be met frequently in the tight and sometimes explosive confines of the jail. As in the case of longshoremen, this joking should also serve as

> An important boundary and symbol of group solidarity... and probably contributes to some unknown degree to the maintenance of this solidarity. This function of joking behaviour was to some degree recognized by Radcliffe-Brown when he stated that the joking relationship is a relation of alliance. (Filcher 1972:112-113)

However, we must point out, as does Filcher, that joking behaviour in the context of the street subcultures does not fit to the end with Radcliffe-Brown's definition since this particular type of joking behaviour is not connected with kinship or the alliance of normally hostile groups. Yet, when this joking behaviour is also directed at the straight group with whom street people interact and have a formally hostile relationship (prison guards or matrons, for instance), it falls in better with Radcliffe-Brown's (1952:106) thesis since its direct equivalent and frequent substitute is as close as the setting allows.

A further example of the part played by folklore in the daily conduct of the street's business are stories comparing *then* and *now, there* and *here,* which serve to give depth and continuity to a lifestyle centred on the immediate and alienating necessities of the addict's life and add to it the dimension of belonging to a *community* expanding over time and space.

Finally, the very strong ethical tenor of some of the anecdotes cannot be overlooked. Although most appear to start as descriptive statements of facts, they often become enmeshed in value judgements. Fidelity between mates is emphatically stressed, "honour among thieves" (as the informants sometimes voice it ironically), the necessity to present a united front to outsiders, love and support, retaliation fairly meted out to transgressors, are not only themes but explicitly stated morals whose message is indistinguishable from the ones carried by tales of the straight world. The values of a "devalued" subculture appear in no way less ethical than those of the larger culture. Through the stories, jokes, and bullshitting events, the same care is exercised in providing warnings against physical danger of all natures, but also, more subtly, in expressing a justification which appears to protect the vulnerability of the group and contribute to the psychological welfare of its individuals.

EMICS *AND* *STEREOTYPES*

The formulation of what Dundes calls "folk fallacies" takes the form of traditional stereotypes. Interestingly, when street people formulate stereotypes they are able to handle several sets of them. Much of the data deals with the manipulation of members of the researcher's culture by the informants, a culture also known to them and of which they have sometimes been a part themselves. These informants' assumption is that they are familiar with both sets of emics. I have used the following labels to differentiate between the nature and attribution of emic information: *straight* is used for the informants' emic view of the researcher's culture, as well as for what the informants assume to be the straight person's own emic views of either culture; and *street* or sometimes *folk* for the informants' emic views and understanding of their own environment.

The insiders' emic view of outsiders often becomes a handy stereotype providing guidelines for proper handling and manipulation of those outsiders. Thus, the stereotypic fabrication of straight people as *greedy* enables street people to act upon this particular characteristic for their own profit. Conversely, straight people's emic view of street people as *irresponsible* and *untrustworthy* enables them to agree with the principles of paternalistic, authoritarian, judicial, and correctional systems.

In Chapter V, a double description takes place: *a folk* stereotype of both street and straight people often accompanied by the *straight* stereotype for both groups: e.g. "You think you are... and that we are... while in fact you are... and we are..." The folk (street emic) description is made to sound of the more convincing ("true") that its contradictory version (straight emic) is also known to the street speaker, thus weakening the straight interlocutor's position. Whereas straight people are, on the whole, only familiar with their own characterization of both groups, street people know both street and straight versions of the exo- and endo-stereotypes.

It is sometimes difficult to ascertain—when the etic interpretation corresponds to a certain extent with a stereotypic definition—whether the etic interpretation is not simply a rationalization of straight people's own emic interpretation. Let us consider, for instance, the common characteristics attributed to the Trickster:

> Violation of taboo, impulsiveness, a lack of close, caring relationships, apparent disregard for the feelings of others, an inability to learn from past mistakes, lack of anxiety or remorse, an exhibitionistic narcissism, constant use of the pretense and trickery, and a demeanour of childlike, innocent charm. (Abrams and Sutton-Smith 1977:30)

Such also appear to be the characteristics frequently possessed by the main character of the personal-experience stories I was told by women of the street. These characteristics will be recognized throughout the texts quoted in Appendix D, but Jo's description of her sister's actions may serve to exemplify briefly these traits:

My sister has robbed my mark a couple of times. He sets up an apartment for me and she goes and cleans it out! The furniture, the colour T.V.... Twice she did that to him!... She would do that to anybody that would give her the opportunity. But, see, I was in here [jail] and I thought I would be getting out on bail. So, he rented me an apartment, and put all kinds of furniture in it, bought a colour T.V. for me... Just everything! It was all waiting for me. I said, "Well, like, I'm going to be a bit,. so you might as well give her a key and she can stay there until I'm sprung." And so he did. He went out of town. He came back a month or two later and the place is empty! She sold everything. So, he did it again! She blows my mind! You know [to her friend sitting beside her] she's dead serious! And they laugh and I laugh too, but for different reasons... She is downtown, she's sick, she can't get any money... She says, "The next guy that walks around the corner, that's it, I'm gonna nail him!" And she will! She'll just punch him in the face, knock him down, take his money and go. [2]

Many of the Trickster's characteristics were also described to me by people professionally involved with these women. In other words, this description of what resembles so-called "psychopathic symptoms" and which is seen as an etic definition appears to be the stereotypic image of street women (and presumably street people at large) held by relatively knowledgeable straight people, a stereotype which also appears to be willingly adopted by street people themselves.

It is my impression that the etic characterization tended to disappear from the narratives as my informants came to know me better. It is not that they had recognized in me someone whose understanding and open-mindedness could easily transcend the gap between us, but simply because the point had already been made clear. They had shown me

---

[2] The informants' syntax and vocabulary have been respected in all the texts quoted here.

that they knew how I saw them. Knowing my culture, they had *conversed* with me on my terms. This point having been established by them, I made the subsequent point: I knew where I stood and had no intention of foolishly pretending that this not where I was going to remain, yet I also sought to understand. The point was not to "become natives or to mimic them," the point was to try and, "in the widened sense of the term in which it encompasses very much more than talk, to converse with them." (Geerts 1973:13)

In the symbiotic relationship involving street and straight people—a symbiosis that justifies perhaps the equal use of etic and emic descriptions by the members of the group under study—they have an advantage over us (it is knowingly that I so clearly draw the line between *them* and *us,* following them in that distinction). I believe that their stereotypes of us are more useful to them than our stereotypes of them are to us: Of necessity, their stereotypes have to be more refined since their dependence on us is greater than our dependence on them, and since they have to try harder at manipulating us than we do them.

CULTURAL BOUNDARIES

Stereotypes mainly serve to reinforce the delineation of cultural boundaries between groups. As *prostitutes* (James 1972a:1-9), as *street addicts* (Agar 1973:2-4, Sutter 1966:180-186), and, as *jail inmates* (Coutts 1961:24-29, Irwin and Cressey 1964), my informants triply fulfill the requirements for membership in a subculture. Their presence in jail, although frequent, is usually of short duration and only comes as a result of their participation in the activities of one or the other two groups: It is only a secondary subculture. They also understand their prostitution activities (or that of their friends when they not themselves "working girls") to be related to the need to support a drug habit. Consequently, their first and foremost integration is into the street addicts' subculture. In fact, a sixteen year old met on the street gave me this unexpected etymology: "We're called hookers because we're hooked."

As members of a subculture, they share many of the values of the larger culture, but they differ from it in their "shared learned behaviours" resulting in "the characteristic ways of thinking and acting which make possible identification as group." (James 1972a:6) Snow, a Tsimshian woman, always referred to her "own people." When questioned, she said she meant "street people, not other Indians." Julie indicated that she and her husband were street people "because of the way we fit in and the things we know." Her statement is the non-scholarly version of Goodenough's definition of culture.

> Whatever it is one has to know or believe in order to operate in a manner acceptable to its member, and to do so in any role that they accept for any of themselves. By this definition, we should note that culture is not a material phenomenon; it does not consist of things, people, behaviour, or emotions. It is rather an organization of those things. It is the form of things that people have in mind, their model for perceiving, relating, and otherwise interpreting them. (Goodenough 1957:167)

As well as share the characteristics and values of their own group, street addicts must also introduce outsiders to the role they are to play in the street socio-economic system. They must do so because the survival of their subculture depends so much on interaction with the larger culture. Newcomers to the street culture, whether as street insiders or straight outsiders, have to be somehow drawn into a continual process of socialization. Some of the things they learn are probably the same: What makes a *rounder* a rounder and *a square* a square, and what can they expect from each other.

As the data were collected and informants talked about what took place on the street between straight and street people, they simultaneously acted out this confrontation by drawing me into it and defining their characteristics as *street* characteristics while *straight* characteristics were seen as being my own. By strictly defining our respective identities and roles, they also established secure boundaries between us. As they described the lifestyle and values of both groups, it became clear that boundaries between them could only be crossed by people who have relinquished their allegiance to their former group. Knowledge of that culture is naturally not forgotten, but may be retrospectively transformed by the adoption of the new culture's values.

Many street people come from straight families and were themselves straight; or a mark may become so involved in a woman's lifestyle that he may end end up adopting her pace and manner of life. Others have crossed the line in reverse. In their transitional state, they may even be named: one of the several definitions given for an *acey-ducey* is "someone who is not on the level. They rock. Like an ex-junkie that comes back for a visit." (Bugsy) Marginal people themselves are useful in determining the boundaries since their exceptional status serves to define the nature of their difference. In spite of the moderate flow from one group to the other, and the symbiotic nature of the ongoing relationship between the two groups, boundaries are firmly maintained.

> Categorical ethnic distinctions do not depend on an absence of mobility, contact, and information but do entail social processes of exclusion and incorporation whereby discrete categories are maintained despite changing participation and membership in the course of individual life histories. Secondly, one finds that stable, persisting, and offer vitally important social relations are maintained across such boundaries, and are frequently based precisely on the dichotomized ethnic status (Barth 1969:10)

But these "categorical ethnic distinctions" are not all that clear cut since, to start with, my informants' definition of straightness was not quite as exclusive as mine. Throughout the research, I had to attempt and divest myself of such reactions as "If her sister is a stripper, her bother is in the Pen, and her parents are God knows where (she does not), how can she claim to have been, until very recently, straight (i.e. like me)?" Thus, it is from the twice-antithetic standpoint of straightness and middle class that the contrasting lifestyles depicted to me had to be analyzed. As the epitome of the straight, I perhaps found it easier to act out my part in our street-straight transactions, symbolizing all the straight values and calling in response for an affirmation of the street values. To this extent, only women who felt challenged and met me at least half way became informants.

Incorporating the interview situation into the ethnography produces data *en abîme,* a well known literary device which reveals a plot within a plot, both held in an analogical relation, and each serving to throw light on the other. The transactions between researcher and informants, with the definition of boundaries to be maintained or transgressed, but always to be acknowledged, are part of an ethnography of communication which encompasses verbal exchanges between two cultures. Throughout the study, the contrast of outlooks will be stressed, as a reiteration of the informants' need for clearly defined boundaries.

THE SETTING

The very setting (the "Street") in which most transactions take place or are initiated is itself viewed differently by the two groups. In Vancouver, the Street can be *downtown* ("Granville, Davie...") or *uptown* ("East Hastings, Cordova, the Stratford [Hotel]..."). Many people, especially drug addicts, concentrate their activities aroundt *the Corner.* The Corner (exclusively a street term) is formed by the intersection of East Hastings and Columbia streets. From a street point of view, the West side of the intersection is quite devoid on interest: it is almost straight. But the North East corner, with the Sunrise Hotel and the adjacent beer parlour in front of which intoxicated or drugged women are sometimes seen taking the early afternoon sun, and the South East corner, with the Cozy Corner, a Chinese grocery store, around which hang expectant junkies and hookers: *that* is The Corner. The name is also extended to include a small neighbouring area (see Appendix C).

To me, the Corner is Hastings and Columbia. It's a name for that whole general area. Down to Carrall, from Pender over to Powell, that whole area. To me, the Street and the Corner are the same. Like, when I'm talking of getting out of here [jail] and hitting the street, it's just get out, but when I talk about the Street, I talk about the Corner. (Dee)

Photograph courtesy of Lincoln Clarkes
(Worldwide Green Eyes).

Julie describes the Street as made of "pawnshops, restaurants, hotels, beer parlours, drugstores, novelty shops." Possibly apart from the pawnshops, at least the highly visible ones, the description would apply equally to uptown and downtown, although the physical appearance of the latter and the type of people it draws put it in definite notch above the former, both from a street and straight point of view.

However, most straight people interviewed make a clear distinction between "downtown" (the centre of which they see as being the intersection of Granville and Georgia streets) and "uptown" (which they usually call "Chinatown" and do not frequent much): "Most people don't go there, there's nothing that draws them there.") . Downtown, they say, there are "department stores, small stores, office buildings, dental and medical buildings, flower and china shops, hotels and theatres." In Chinatown (or *uptown* in Julie's term), they list the old Library, Chinese and Japanese curio shops, Chinese restaurants and markets, and the Police Station. One person also added "and porno shops." Two young men also mentioned the Traffic Court. Two years earlier, this might have been my description,[3] that of an ordinary straight person who, just as Julie or the people quoted, only sees what is relevant to his or her experience.

The only additions brought by the other informants to Julie's list of beer parlours, drugstores, hotels, restaurants, and novelty shops were sexual aids are bought, were theatres showing X-rated films and, in the case of some *boosters,* several department stores know for their shoplifting opportunities. Obviously, the informants' mental map of the city is reduced to the occupationally relevant parts of the street, their working and living areas.

---

[3] In the Spring of 1975, I was asked by the British Columbia Police Commission to write a report on street prostitution (Layton 1975). One of the first things I did was go out at night with street workers from the Gastown Team, an organization concerned with the protection of juveniles, who patrol the areas described as "uptown" and "downtown." It was a total revelation: The nocturnal streets became almost a photographic negative of the streets I knew by day. Shops disappeared and between those vanished storefronts stared the unsuspected openings of innumerable walk-up hotels and rooms for rent: no lobby, just a door and a steep staircase. The same phenomenon also gave substance to the people who come to life at night and make shadows of the straight people left over from the day.

Not only do the two groups' perception of the physical reality of the two areas differ, but it is also clear from the responses elicited from the straight persons interviewed, whatever their area of residence of work, that they have a more extensive vision of Vancouver. The same point is well illustrated by Orleans (1967), mentioned in Could and White (1974:34-47), which gives the characteristics example of the three maps of Los Angles perceived through the eyes of (a) upper middle class whites in Westwood, (b) black residents of Avalon, and (c) Spanish-speaking residents of Boyle Heights. In these maps, the city is gradually reduced in size to the extent, in the Boyle Heights case, of only including their immediate area, City Hall, and the bus depot, "the major entrance and exit to their tiny urban world."

Straight people who go to town to work or shop express few feelings about it. Either they "like it" or they "don't like what *they've* done with," usually referring to its physical appearance. Street people, on the other hand, draw much of their strength from the very environment of the street where their transactions take place, from knowing it, and being known as a part of it. Brandy puts it this way:" Lots of people can't go from Burrard to Davie. They go crazy. It's another territory. They're afraid of people, they can't fend for themselves."

The well-defined areas in which street addicts feel at home also reflect their own status in the recognized hierarchy of the street. This is even more true of addict streetwalkers, whose choice of area is not only regulated by primary factors related to their addiction (type of drug they use, their involvement in the drug scene, whether they are also traffickers, etc.) but also secondary factors related to their prostitution (their physical appearance, grooming, remuneration expected for services, etc.) Sue pointed out that "the Granville street girls think they're better than the Stratford girls, the Stratford girls think they're better than the Hastings street girls." But, wherever its exact location, the Street is for all the informants, more than a physical reality: It is a way of life. As addicts, they recognize and adapt to their own favourite spot the feelings Dee attributed to her friends at the Corner, "You can take a hype at the Corner, and they can live down there and be content or happy, or whatever, and they can live down there without needing the rest of the world."

SUMMARY

The following ethnographic description of the various types of verbal transactions in which street women engage draws on three main approaches: The concepts of *ethnosemantics* (Goodenough 1957, Burling 1969, Sturtevant 1964, Frake 1969, Black 1974:521-529), of *symbolic interaction* (Goffman 1959, 1961, 1963; McCall and Simmons 1966) and on an analysis of the *folklore* (Abrahams, 1968, Dundes 1971, Cochran 1974). It is essentially an ethnography of communication, with attempts to define the boundaries of the community where specific speech acts occur, the nature of these exchanges, and the various codes adopted in these encounters.

Like the works of James (1971), Agar (1973), and Spradley (1970, 1975), this work focuses on an essentially emic interpretation. The consideration of a deviant subculture previously described by social scientists becomes irrelevant here, since the only deviance acknowledged by the informants is that of members of their own culture who fail to conform to the expected behaviour pattern within the group and endanger its cohesiveness: the *rats* and the *rip offs.*

The informants' understanding of their socio-economic environment directs their transactions with members of the larger culture and among themselves. Their economic survival depends on their management of members of the other culture, while their social survival depends on their management of relationships within their own group. Furthermore, the inclusion of the informant-researcher transaction into the study permits the consideration of a double process: It describes the informant's interaction with a member of the straight culture, an interaction usually seen as mutually exploitative, and illustrates the informant's method of imparting and defining a cultural value system.

CHAPTER TWO

FIELDWORK AND THE INTERVIEW SITUATION

In the course of a past study undertaken for the British Columbia Police Commission (B.C.P.C.) and during the present research, I talked to about two dozen women, prostitutes and heroin addicts. The actual fieldwork took two different forms: I first became acquainted with the setting as an observer, and I proceeded later to interview women whose transactions normally take place in the same setting.

PAST AND PRESENT FIELDWORK

I was retained in 1975 by B.C.P.C. to produce a report on street prostitution and during that Summer I spend two or three nights a week in the areas described earlier as *downtown* and *uptown*. I accompanied individual street workers on their rounds usually from 9 p.m. to midnight or later, and on a few occasions I walked or drove around with a policeman detached to the street workers' team. A member of the Morality Squad and a member of the gay community also introduced me, separately, to some places outside the working area of the street workers. Through these people I became acquainted with specific locations I would have been at a loss to penetrate on my own. Through them I became acquainted with significant street corners, whole city blocks, hotels, beer parlours, and bars or discotheques reputed to cater to groups with specialized interests such as juvenile homosexuals, black pimps, or drug traffickers. I sometimes returned to these places later, and in time became more familiar with them and more sensitive to actions or signals, and even to sounds specific to some of them. During that Summer, I obtained some understanding of the physical environment familiar to my informants.

I also sat in on trials or read trial transcripts of cases which related to events relevant to street life: charges of soliciting, living of the avails of prostitution, rape, trafficking, drug related offences, and even one drug related murder. The common enough offences introduced me to another aspect of the informants' life: the judicial and correctional one. The unusual ones introduced me to events that sometimes became part of the street folklore (e.g. Porky and the Mafia story, Chapter Four).

However, for the actual interviews and the new texts obtained, I relied almost exclusively for the present study on information gathered in Oakalla, the Lower Mainland Regional Correctional Centre, from the Spring to the Winter of 1976. The main reason for this new selection was that in 1975 I had not thought I would later be using for a dissertation the data I was collecting for the report. Also, information given to me as a researcher for the Police Commission might not have been forthcoming had the informants known it would be used later to further a personal goal. Moreover, the direction of the research was different. In essence, the work done in 1975 simply became one of familiarization with the setting and the lifestyle of individuals I would be interviewing a year or so later.

From a practical and personal point of view, I preferred jail interviews to street work. Unlike Jennifer James, who spent many nights talking to her prostitute informants in little cafes, at home, and in a variety of places outside the jail where she had often first met them, I found this forthright and self-assured approach incompatible with my own character. I formed a seemingly good relationship with at least four of my informants, but there was never the slightest pretence that it would be carried outside the jail. One of them offered to meet me after her release, but her activities immediately absorbed her (I heard later than she was "misbehaving again") and we never met.

I did not attempt either to talk to unknown women on the street when they were working, even before I came to know a little more about street life, and certainly saw it as in impossibility afterwards. Part of this reluctance is due to a natural shyness and a lack of personal salesmanship. The knowledge that I would be interfering with street business (usually *hooking),* the implicit patronization contained in my assumption that I might question them, the understanding that they would have to reject this public approach if only for appearance's sake, did not encourage me to consider this method a desirable one. Most of my reluctance, however, was due to the fact that I could find no answer to the question: "Why would they *want* to talk to me?"

In 1975, I was sometimes introduced to street women by police officers or street workers. This was also an unacceptable method, since the women had very little choice to refuse (only one did) and the person who performed the introduction was also present during the interview. From these brief and rather unsatisfactory encounters, I only retained for the present research the odd remark which struck me as an unsolicited meaningful statement, a challenge, an assertion of self worth, etc. (c.g. Bonnie, when our detective go-between had left for a minute, saying, perhaps to break the silence, "Last night, I made 500 dollars!" I understood this statement to be a challenge and answered, "Wow, that's more than I make in a month!" This answer momentarily denied whatever presumption I might have felt to interview her in a police car. My status was better than hers at the time and for the occasion (researcher for the Police Commission as opposed to junkie hooker who was in no position to refuse a cop's request), but in terms that we could both appreciate, we had established that she was otherwise "better" than me.

Private interviews in jail were the only method I could envisage as a sensible possibility. Many researchers have mentioned that people seem willing to talk while they are in jail. Among my informants, I guessed at many reasons for that willingness: boredom for some, and perhaps a desire for the more docile to do what they thought was expected of them; sheer enjoyment, after a reluctant beginning, of being appreciated as a story teller; intellectual challenge for those who stressed their education ("I started one term at Langara *[Community College]*"; "I finished grade 12 in here *[jail])*" to try and explain in the terms they assumed to be those of the researcher how street life differed from straight life and how much more exciting it all was; and, for at least one, the interviews were seen as a didactic exercise. In all cases, the practice of *bullshitting* as an art form took precedence over whatever other reasons they might have had for agreeing to talk to me.

The authorities were generous with me, giving me one of their few available offices, and free access to any inmates I chose to interview. I was not a total stranger, since I had held previous interviews in jail and had also been given a letter of introduction from the Chairman of the Police Commission. I had also sent them a copy of my 1975 report on prostitution. However, I was now engaged in this new research as a private individual, so I very much appreciated their courtesy.

Jail interviews may leave much to be desired. None puts it more scathingly than Polsky.

> We know also, or ought to know by now, that data gathered from caught criminals, for reasons in addition to and quite apart from possible sampling bias, are not only very partial but partially suspect. These are data that are much too heavily retrospective, data from people who aren't really free to put you down; data often involving the kind of "cooperativeness" in which you get told what the criminal thinks you want to hear so you will yep off his back or may be do him some good with the judge or parole board; data from someone who is not behaving as he normally would in his normal life situations; and

above all, data that you cannot supplement with, or interpret in the light of your direct observation of the criminal's behavior in his natural environment (Polsky 1969: 115-116).

One can counter some of the reasons given by Polsky for condemning the validity of data thus gathered:

1. Data are not necessarily to be shunned because they are "retrospective." Indeed, most data, except those arising from direct observation or participation, are of a retrospective nature. They are also processed and selected data and serve to provide an insight into emic values and emphases, and the constructs of reality (Whittaker 1973). Narratives are seldom bare statements of facts but usually give explanations for events. It is as such that these retrospective data are useful since, as Schwartz and Merton mention in a passage quoted by Whittaker (1973:7):

> Talk about motives does not end with the suggestion that it is the "real" or "true" reason for the act in question but taps the moral vocabulary through which the informant appraises and evaluates myriads actions and relationships.

Moreover, the individual manner of accounting is in itself revealing of the informant's attempts at presenting a front congruent with his or her self-image and believed to be acceptable to the researcher. (Scott and Lyman 1968)

2. The simple comparison of street lifestyle and straight lifestyle is the most potent put-down some informants can conceive. It is also a socially acceptable one since, as the saying goes, "there's nothing personal in it." Unless, of course; one *chooses* to make it so and acknowledges both the put-down and one's inclusion in the decried group.

3.   The "cooperativeness" is in itself an event worthy of investigation. As will be seen later, it is a well-recognized phenomenon.

4   My scepticism has grown considerably about the ability of the straight researcher to come close enough to the subject's—especially the criminal subject's—"scene" to analyze the latter's behaviour in the light of his experience of this scene. Naturally, exceptions have to be made for people who belong to it or have come close enough to it, like the Milners for the black pimps (1972) for instance, Polsky for the hustlers (1967), or Becker for the professional musicians (1951). But, can these people be said to be entirely straight any longer?

I am quite aware that this scepticism is a result of the *bullshitting* to which I was subjected, and the reiteration that square Johns simply cannot "understand" street people. I consider it a part of my socialization as a square John. In other words, "I know my place." Since street people and squares often interact and feed on each other, the revelation of the former's culture to the latter is important, as well as the understanding of the role assigned to them by this culture.

THE INFORMANTS

The Population
The first part of my 1975 report to the B.C.P.C. drew on the court, police, and probation files of one hundred women arrested between 1973 and 1975 in Vancouver for "soliciting for the purpose of prostitution." The number was arbitrarily selected, but the files were chosen on the basis of fullness. Thus, a young girl for whom the court had requested a thorough pre-sentence report was as likely to be represented as a woman with a heavy criminal record, well known by the police, and who may have been on a long probation.

This biased sample may also not have been representative of the actual age distribution on the street, since information on girls under the age of seventeen had to be sought separately. The manner in which information had been gathered did not present a great consistency either and some files did not even touch upon aspects very well documented in other (e.g. family background). Some files were ten or fifteen years old, and fashion, trends, and emphases in data collection were sometimes discernible (one file, for instance, considered the women's early childhood and toilet training; I also noticed the sudden disappearance of religious affiliation from the data gathered). With these serious caveats, an attempt was made to collect information related to the women's personal history, their family background and home environment, their involvement with various types of drugs, their medical and psychiatric history, court history (rather than criminal history which may not always have been formally sanctioned with arrest and trial), and their occupational history. These women form the general population from which the informants for this dissertation were drawn, and a summary of the report's findings, which were consistent with the Limoges survey (1967), may serve as a useful if very sketchy introduction.

The youngest woman included in the report was 14 years old and the oldest one 45; but most of the ages ranged between 16 and 24. Of the thirty who reported when they entered prostitution, 80 percent indicated that it was before the age of 20, peaking at 16-18. Most were Caucasian, and of the twelve Native women in the sample, eight were between the ages 15 and 19. They came almost equally from urban and rural areas, and almost two thirds of them were from British Columbia. A few did not go beyond elementary school and a few others completed secondary school, but the majority left school somewhere between grades 8 and 11. The occupations they had intermittently held ranged from waitresses to clerks or strippers. Many had never held legitimate employment and most were on Welfare.

Some of the women arrested had been married and were usually divorced or separated. A few lived with an "old lady" in a lesbian relationship, but most lived with an "old man" in a common-law relationship. The "old man" usually had a criminal record, made his living by trafficking or other illegitimate means, and was most often a heroin addict. Those of the women who were not themselves heroin addicts had worked or were working for a white or a black pimp. Many of them (30 per cent) had had one or two children, often given up for adoption at birth; the few who had kept them usually had them looked after by a relative.

More than half of the women's early home life had been affected by their parents' divorce or separation, by the death or desertion of one parent, or some other family disruption. Fourteen were reported to be illegitimate or to have been adopted in infancy. Many reported leaving home before the age of 15.

One quarter came from small families of one or two children, more than half came from families with between three and six children, and the rest came from very large families of seven, ten, or even more children. Almost a third of the sixty-four women for whom the information was available were first-born children. It was also noted that when the family had to bear the pressure of a severe additional problem (a blind mother, a mother slowly dying of cancer, a brother with Down syndrome, a badly crippled parent, a sister with cerebral palsy, or a mother with psychiatric problems), in half the cases the first-born child was part of the sample. Moreover, eight of them were the eldest daughter in families of five to nine children.

Almost half of the home environments were described as "average." An almost equal number were described as "bad" (alcoholic parents, abused children, etc.). The files substantiated seven cases of molestation by a close male relative before the age of 10, and suspected two more. A small number of women were reported by social workers or probation officers as coming from a punitive or extremely religious family, often among foster parents.

The parents' work history showed on the whole an attempt at keeping more or less steady employment as labourers or semi-skilled workers. A small group showed only sporadic employment, odd jobs, and social assistance. At the other pole, an even smaller group indicated parents with a professional and middle class background.

Only half of the women arrested for soliciting on the street and in bars were heroin addicts. All, however, used some type of drug, whether alcohol, barbiturates, marijuana, LSD, speed, cocaine, etc. The younger girls still reported sniffing glue. Among the heroin addicts, daily consumption was anything from a light habit of two to three caps to an expensive habit of six to eight caps or more of low quality drug. Quite a few were or had been on a methadone maintenance program.

Nearly half the women had never been charged with or convicted of soliciting before but may have received several "warnings" under an earlier section of the *Criminal Code*. The other half had at least one conviction for the same offence and many had four or five previous soliciting convictions. Most other convictions were for trafficking or being in possession of narcotics. Three quarters of the women had also been convicted of petty theft. Some of the younger women had been involved in crimes which were until recently mostly committed by men, such as car theft or breaking and entering, and more cases of assaults were reported among the juveniles.

The underground prostitution of call girls and housewives was not the object of the study and only visible prostitution figured in the 1975 report. I distinguished between three general zones of operation: Skid Road (*Uptown* in the present study, see Appendix C), the Granville street area, and the Davie street area. In the first area, where The Corner and the Stratford Hotel figure prominently, the proportion of heroin addicts was overwhelming. Lower fees were routinely charged and the economic rule of thumb, where one trick corresponded to one cap, was usually applied. I understand that, for a variety of legal and economic reasons, prostitution downtown had recently been more obvious, more aggressive, and, reputedly under the guidance of pimps, was proliferating. I did not believe that street prostitution among the junkies of the first area had been noticeably modified by the changes reported elsewhere. If the addict prostitutes' business was affected by the competition coming from the increased number of prostitutes reported by the Police and the news media, they must simply have resorted to more thefts, more con jobs, and those who did not traffic before would perhaps now have to do so.

Individual Informants

The informants selected for the new 1978 study came essentially from the general population described above. The only criterion of inclusion in this new group was that the women *know* the street. For the Oakalla prison staff drawing up the list, it meant women usually known to be users, traffickers, and/or prostitutes, whatever their present charge might be. The informants were selected in a casual manner: The staff looked at a list of inmates and put a check mark in front of those whose experience was appropriate and added: "This one would probably talk to you ... that one might ..." From the checked names I then selected one who was called to the office where I sat. The informants often asked how they had been selected, in which case I explained that I had picked their name at random from a list I had been given of people who might be "interesting" to talk to (rather than "willing" to talk to me, which would have been seen as a put down), and that I did not know anything about them personally.

For a variety of reasons, the main one being obviously the informants' good will and accessibility, ten women were selected as informants. Their ages ranged between 21 and 33, with a mean of 25.8 years. Only two had not travelled farther than Alberta; the experience of the others, as addicts and prostitutes, covered most of Canada and part of the United States; and three had also been overseas. Two were fairly new to the street, the other eight had been involved in it since their late teens or earlier. All but one had been in prison before, some many times. Three had requested to be held in Protective Custody for their own protection and they lived together in one room where everybody often joined in the conversation. Two others were first interviewed together, then broke up their relationship and were afterwards seen separately. The last three were always seen alone. Some informants claimed or denied areas of expertise (e.g. "I've never been a working girl, but I've been trafficking since I was sixteen," Dee). The final criterion of inclusion was whether or not the woman *herself* accepted her definition as belonging among "street people."

All around the jail, I recognized the sounds and smells of an English mental hospital where I worked twenty-five years earlier, and some of the listlessness and the restlessness were also the same. All the informants, but Boots who had just arrived, had the pasty complexion and the shuffling gait of the institutionalized. They all wore the same jeans and the same T-shirts, yet some said that they were pleased that they no longer had to wear uniforms. They all had jewellery and most exhibited tattoos. The definitions, jokes, boasts, and fears quoted in the next chapters and in Appendix D are extracted from rambling conversations held with Bugsy, Brandy, Snow, Julie, Jo, Sue, Sugar, Tiny, and Boots.

I never saw their files and only knew what they told me and how—very subjectively—I related to them. When Dee and Bugsy, my first informants, came into my office and agreed to talk to me, I became part of their culture, along with the other square people who interact with them in a complex system of communication and exchange. As a newcomer to their culture, I had to learn a certain behaviour. I could never be *solid*, but could I be taught to be *good people* rather than *ignorant?* What minimum knowledge would I have to acquire in order to understand the rough guidelines of our transactions? What would be my place in their order of things? I did not know anything and I had to be sounded out and then taught.

BUGSY was the youngest, a pale girl of 21 with dyed blond hair. From one interview to the next, I did not know how I would find her: boisterous, sulky, funny, apparently pleased to see me, or barely civil. Yet, she always came and she always stayed. She described herself as physically and mentally tough and often talked of beatings received and given, of the utter pitilessness of street life, and of surviving it all, and coming out a winner. I found her a delightful storyteller. In spite of her age, she had been a hooker and a junkie for eight years. Reading my notes a year later, I could only remember her as young and disarming. I once asked her whether I could greet her if I happened to meet her on the street after her release. She looked sideways and said, "You don't know me."

DEE was a stolid and sturdily built woman. Her composure was always admirable and she exuded strength and common sense. She had always been a lesbian and at the beginning always came with Bugsy. Dee was a junkie, a trafficker, and talked of robberies, escapes, and violence. I thought her brave, found her courteous, and felt considerable respect for her. She also applied systematically to our interviews the conning techniques she was at the same time describing for me. After four months, I said: "We can go no further. You now know more about me than I know about you." She agreed politely, and that was that.

BRANDY, at 33, was the oldest of my informants. I thought her an unwise and indiscreet woman: After twenty-two years on the street and in the jails, she still talked to the wrong people and said the wrong things; she was in Protective Custody. Her long experience in American and Canadian streets and jails made her an ideal subject, equally fluent in street argot, standard language, and medico-legal jargon. She was unfortunately moody, with a very short attention span and interviewing her amounted to an endurance test. We often sat out in the Protective Custody enclosure where she sunbathed, forever distracted by the male inmates working nearby. Although a junkie, her self-professed worst enemy was alcohol: She could never resist it and had "blackouts" during which she beat people senseless. Her violence was also directed at herself and her forearms were entirely covered with slash scars. She could express herself in the foulest way imaginable, yet was ceremoniously polite with me. I think she found me somewhat "simple" and totally inconsequential.

SNOW was a beautiful Tsimshian girl of 24, with remarkably fine hands. Since these portraits are purely subjective and impressionistic, I shall say that I saw Bugsy and Snow as "girls" and the others as "women." I saw them both as sentimental, vulnerable, and in need of protection perhaps against themselves more than anything else. In spite of their having an experience of life that I could not even fathom, I saw them both as children. Snow had been involved in many petty activities and thefts, small-time trafficking, and also supported herself by prostitution. Like Bugsy, she was impulsive and had an almost uncontrollable wildness about her. Two weeks before the end of her term, she escaped.

JULIE said she came from a straight family. She was married and had a child of whom we often talked and who was born in jail during a previous term of imprisonment. Her husband was also serving a sentence in Oakalla. She gave me the impression that she practiced a somewhat higher class of prostitution than the others, that all her activities were in fact superior to that of the other inmates, and she mentioned that she and her husband had "worked" in England and done well. She had luminous grey eyes in a heart shaped face and her appearance and manner would support her claim that her greatest success was with marks. She always showed interest in my work and enjoyed discussing a great variety of topics. This was probably another aspect of the insistence with which she projected a "superior" image.

JO was a very composed, handsome, intelligent, and often bitter woman. She had travelled to England and North Africa and was interested to hear that I had lived a long time in Morocco, a country she had liked. She prostituted herself as a last resort and preferred to boost or steal from her customers.

BOOTS was small and quite childlike in appearance, with long blond hair. She had been well protected by her old man and, after his death, went to work for a white pimp who got her off heroin for a while. Although a prostitute and drug addict of long standing, she had only recently entered street life. She told tales of success unrivalled by the other women, and her contribution figures mostly in Appendix D.

SUE, with Dee the only informant who was not a prostitute, was mostly a trafficker and booster, who started using at the age of 13. She was an unfriendly woman and sometimes attempted to intimidate me. These minor power struggles were neither important nor frequent enough to prevent her from talking to me. She was a precise informant who took the trouble to correct my misapprehensions.

TINY and SUGAR were the only two informants who appeared unable to cope with the pressure of their personal life. They had both been straight and unable to resist the temptation of a more "exciting" life, but neither appeared to have been very successful on the street.

During the nine months of my fieldwork, Tiny and Jo were released; Bugsy and Boots were transferred; Sue, Snow, and Brandy escaped. Brandy was recaptured soon afterwards and said it had been "worth it!" All were junkies, all made their living on the street, and all would probably go back to it after their release or their escape, as they had always done in the past.

These women are not part of the hard core of often prestigious inmates who are unwilling to talk to non-officials. Those are seen on the street as *solid* or *heavies* and often become in jail the mediators between other inmates and the staff. They use their strength and ability to manipulate people, grant favours and protection, mete out punishment, and find that their authority is seldom challenged. They are usually junkies with a "name" on the street, who find that their reputation has preceded them in jail. They would have had no reason to speak to me and would have gained nothing from it. Of all my informants, Dee was the only one who had a strength of character and personality comparable to theirs. Referring perhaps to the women I interviewed, Dee once explained that it was not "very cool to help straight people," and I later came to see their willingness to be interviewed as a flaw in the composite picture of cultural competence they were otherwise building for me. This flaw was somewhat redeemed by my absolute certainly that they would never have spoken to me on the street.

THE INTERVIEW TRANSACTION

Since the informants' agreement to collaborate had to be solicited before any further step could be taken, our first interview was almost a storming session, where I went very rapidly through what Olesen and Whittaker describe as the first three phases of role-making: surface encounters, proffering (definitions of one's self and the other), and inviting (definitions of both from the informants), selecting and modifying (meaningful and viable portions of researcher's and informant's role). (Olesen and Whittaker 1967:273-281)

I introduced myself and indicated my affiliations, stating that I was neither a social worker nor a psychologist. It was one way to dissociate myself from the overly familiar. I soon realized that this was a necessity. My door was open when I was not interviewing anyone, and after having seen me a few times while waiting to be admitted to the Classification Office across the hall, some women sometimes wandered in and questioned me. Most, having satisfied themselves that I was not what they thought I was (either a psychologist or a social worker, since that particular office was sometimes used by them) left it at that. Others sat on the edge of the desk, ready to flee should I become demanding (or perhaps talk too much), and tried to find out what I was. Since these talks were not formal interviews (i.e. *they* had initiated the interaction, were in control and asking the questions, had not agreed to "talk" to me, decided when they should leave, etc.) they often proved to be profitable conversations where I could observe a free handling of the street-straight encounter. I often noticed that a smoothly running and casual conversation could become diffident and stilted when it turned into a formal interview ("Well, would you like to talk to me?" "Yeah ... O.K...") or could even appear to come to an end until "next time we meet," while in fact continuing to ramble on for some time afterwards. The commitment involved in the change of status for the informant and the pressure for the still inexperienced interviewer seemed to take on a nearly paralyzing quality for both.

Since the informants knew very well—each in her own way—how to handle a social worker or a psychologist, it was a novelty for them to face such an unknown quantity as me, and their incursion into this less familiar territory was interesting to observe. For casual visitors and regular informants, I practised a few definitions of anthropology which would set it apart from their familiar experience. I tried: "As anthropologists, we do not actually take sides. For us, nothing is really "good" or "bad." If it works, it's good, if it doesn't, it's bad." Some may have recognized in this what is partly their own philosophy. Others may have though anthropologists somewhat wishy-washy. But, even if they did not believe me, it was at least a clear departure from what they consider the "preaching" of social workers or the attempt to "get into my head and set me straight" on the part of psychologists.

Before they could decide whether to talk to me, I also had to ask: "So, you may wonder what's in it for you and what's in it for me?" I explained that I was working for my Ph.D. at the university and that my last hurdle was to write a thesis. Their responses would contribute to my research and enable me to write it and then complete my work. I added, "What's in it for you? I can't really pay you. All I can do is leave a "token of my appreciation" or a "consultant's fee" on your account when I have finished, but it won't be very much. On the other hand, some people enjoy talking about what they know and what they're good at ... There's something else which I think is important and it's simply to try and make people understand a little better what goes on. I know most of you really want to be left alone *[vigorous nods of agreement]*, but if the people who make the laws don't know anything about you, your problems, and your needs, the laws are going to reflect that ignorance. I can give you two examples of how a little understanding has improved things: As you know, it is no longer illegal to be a homosexual and, very soon now, someone who presses charges for rape will not be asked whether she is a hooker or not. She will not first have to stand trial on *that* before her case is heard." I always received a strong positive reaction to that last argument since it has long been a very sore point for street women who seldom even bother to press charges for that particular reason.[4] I went on: "Hookers here would prefer to be left alone, too, but it is not the case everywhere else, where they are trying to form unions and to get their problems recognized. *They* are the ones who come out and want to talk about it. They even go on strike sometimes!"

During the first interviews, I explained that I was interested in language and how people describe their life experience, giving the example of what a "bastard" cop would mean to a street woman and a "bastard" prof to a student: How they would describe two different behaviours with the same term and how this term and the behaviour implied would be understood differently by a street woman or by a student, even if neither had an immediate understanding of her street or university counterpart's experience, but knowing what the term meant for her own group. I concluded that "the cop and the prof are probably bastards for the same reasons, but they act it out differently." I also mentioned that I was interested to see how we protected ourselves from such behaviour.

I also found it necessary to explain at some length my interest in language, since my first superficial introduction by a third party as "someone interested in street language" had elicited the amused and patronizing reaction: "You mean "fuck" and stuff like that?"

As an indirect way of checking their familiarity with the environment of the street drug addict, I showed them eight extracts of Agar's, Sutter's, and Preble and Casey's studies, asking them whether they agreed with the illegitimate and criminal procedures described and the terminology used. The latter was thought to differ slightly at times from their own,

---

[4] The following exchange is somewhat typical of feelings expressed by many informants when faced with the implication the prostitutes cannot be raped (I met the defendant in 1975):
Defense counsel: Had you had sex with anybody for money? *Defendant:* I mean, what are you bringing all this up for? I didn't ask to get beat up. I didn't ask to get treated like that. Just because I was a working girl, he can go around, pointing guns and treating me like that? Yes, I have been a working girl. That's what you're asking! Yes, I admit to that. But that does not have to be right for him to force me into that, and pull a gun, and threaten to kill me, does it? Does it? (Vancouver rape trial transcript).

but they totally agreed with the descriptive part of the works. One of them, who was not familiar with the confidence game known as "the hot T.V. game" (Agar 1973:46-47 and see Appendix F), found it so plausibly described that she said, only half jokingly, I think, she might try it after her release from jail.

In the same manner, I sometimes showed James's dissertation to my informants and checked her classification against their own. At the beginning of several interviews, I had James's and Agar's works in evidence on my desk, to establish clearly the fact that such information as I sought from them was in fact already known and not at all of a confidential nature. It is at that point that I also had to explain the crucial difference between *informants* and *informers*.

Pseudonyms

I told them that their anonymity would be respected as much as possible. I could have distorted the data to ensure complete anonymity, but have done nothing beyond the vagueness of the above portraits and the attribution of pseudonyms, mainly for two reasons. Since the informants were called into my office through the classification office, the staff knew who my most frequent visitors were; moreover, and this was by far the most important point (and the reason for which they showed so little interest in preserving their anonymity) the data I collected were totally unimportant from their point of view.

While working for the Police Commission, I once asked a woman if she did nor mind being seen getting out of what was obviously an unmarked police car (others, perhaps less sure of their reputation, had shown some reluctance about it). She answered: "I don't really mind. They know me. They know I wouldn't say anything important!" There was very little doubt as to who "they" were, and could only assume that something "important" would be information on criminal activities (whether knowledge of a crime, its perpetrators, the whereabouts of an escaped convict, or anything which would help the police). This would be *ratting out* on other street people and one would have to have a very good reason for agreeing to do so. The information given to the curious square John—even one endowed with some scholarly title and bent on some scholarly task—was of the same type as the tidbits given to the mark: neither really mattered. But since the point of view of the women and that of the researcher (or the mark) were not the same, the presumed trivia offered by the former may have been all that was wanted from them.

On the second or third interview, I would come back to the question of anonymity already briefly mentioned during the first one. All the informants said that they did not care about it. The implication was that only what they considered important was important. By the same token, it made me a collector of trivia. I insisted on their need for a pseudonym because I was keeping an open dictionary which was available to them and where they could always check their own definitions and comments, as well as those made by other people, and discuss these. I made the double point that they might be embarrassed to have their statements read by other people in the jail, and that their anonymity was also for my protection since I only wanted to know them by a nickname and be unable to identify them later (they indeed often questioned me on "Who said that?"). I was also interested in the types of nicknames they would choose. Only half of them chose their own pseudonyms: Sugar (after consulting Brandy who, with one glance at her well endowed friend, suggested "Grapefruit"), Brandy, Boots, Bugsy (second choice, Tiny being already taken and her own nickname being too well known), and Julie. I selected the others. Thus, because of my insistence and in spite of their own lack of interest, my informants were given pseudonyms. All but one, who righteously insisted that she had no reason to "hide herself." A few days later, in the course of a gossipy session with Brandy, it suddenly became clear that this woman's real name was quite unknown on the street where she was only known by her nickname. Her real name was in fact the best pseudonym she could have used.

My open-mindedness was sometimes tested, as, for instance, when Bugsy and Dee showed me that they were involved in a lesbian relationship. They had both been called to my office together: their names followed each other on the list and I had asked the counselor whether they got on well and could be interviewed together. She had simply answered, "Yes, it will be all right, they're friends." They immediately established their relationship by sitting in front of my desk and holding hands. This first clue having been received in a matter-of-fact fashion, Dee then lit a cigarette which Bugsy sometimes took away from her mouth or her hand and from which she drew two or three times before giving it back to her. There was a half full package on the desk in front of Dee, so their sharing was not to be understood as due to the scarcity of cigarettes. Moreover, taking a cigarette away from someone is a much more intimate gesture than being given one. Dee being quite obviously the dominant individual in this relationship (whatever the nature of it might have been), Bugsy's gesture denoted a trust and intimacy not justifiable by any other type of relationship. This second clue having been accepted, they proceeded to the next one: Dee sat back more comfortably in her hard chair and lifted her legs to let them rest on Bugsy's lap. Throughout the rest of the interview Bugsy massaged Dee's big toes. They also introduced the word *nichey,* grinning and stressing the word so that I would ask what it meant. Dee explained that it referred to anything that aroused one sexually and Bugsy laughed: "Dee is nichey about her big toe!" What made the incident meaningful was that in none of their following interviews did they ever touch each other again and I assume that the whole performance only served as a test. The only other allusion to their relationship occurred during a discussion on tattoos, when Bugsy showed me how her ex-old man's initials had been turned into Dee's initials. When, two months later, I asked Bugsy what were the advantages of having an "old lady" in jail, I felt I had committed a small breach of etiquette since she had never said anything explicit about her first hand knowledge of the situation. I ended my sentence to indicate that the question was not a personal one. She then talked freely of her future plans with Dee.

Once our relationship was established, I sometimes brought them flowers from my garden, cigarettes, chocolate, or gum. Bugsy always brought tea to our interviews, and I felt she was thus establishing a hostess-guest relationship between us. I always brought cigarettes or soft drinks when invited for dinner. I also acknowledged the fact that I had no rights and depended entirely on their good will and hospitality. When introduced by the staff, who sometimes forgot to indicate this clearly, I added: "If you feel like talking to me, that is."

It could be said that I was attempting to allow my informants as much self respect and freedom as they could have in these surroundings, and that by stressing their hospitality and good will I also acknowledged the inequality of the exchange of important (to me) data for only a few dollars or a bunch of lilac. It was such an easy position to assume that I could not truthfully detect what part fraudulence and manipulation took place in the front I was managing, particularly since that front was most naturally suited to my personality. Thus, it could perhaps be argued that sounding respectful and being nice was a con game. Having assumed that this attitude would be acceptable, that my recognition of their courtesy would be appreciated, that became my game.

A parenthesis is necessary to explain the meaning of the word *game*. Of the different meanings attributed Eric Partridge in his *Dictionary of the Underworld* (1950), my informants commonly used two definitions: (1) The quality of having mastered, or having the aptitude to master, techniques for getting money or one's own way through the manipulation of human emotions, and (2) any game in which money and personal gain are the objects, including all hustle and "legitimate" big money enterprises. They know the other definitions: (3) *The Game* or the "pussy game," meaning prostitution, and (4) *High game,* e.g. "When you give ten cents' worth for twenty cents and the trick thinks he got thirty cents' worth." The last two are seem as American or more specifically black American expression or "nigger talk."

It is also evident that some straight-street encounters can be seen as "games" in a more orthodox way, since it holds true in these encounters that

>At least one of the interactants is aware or capable of being made aware that, in realizing his aims in an

encounter, he must take into account the others' expectations of what he expects of them, and vice versa (Scott and Lyman 1970:95).

Furthermore, these encounters may also become "face games," in the words of Goffman, in which "defensive" (self-protective) and "protective" objectives are sought in protecting one participant's identity against damage or spoilage (Scott and Lyman 1970:97). They are all aspects of the game which were familiar to my informants. The game was also enhanced by their awareness that it was also seen as such by many of the straight people who interviewed them in their professional capacity.

BOUNDARIES

Throughout most of the interviews and with most of the informants, two sets of boundaries emerged: those resulting from the confrontation of the two cultures, and those created by the situation itself and the way it had been defined.

In the first case, the cultural straight-street boundaries were double: The customary opposition between straight and street values were reflected in the contrasted characterization of street informants and straight researcher, but a second opposition was also established between straight and street women.

In the second case, the type of data sought was mostly linguistic and dealt with conflict situations: I had not expressed any interest in confidential matters or, explicitly at least, in occupational (i.e. sexual) information. Thus, the overt introduction of the topic of sexual practices in our interviews went beyond the boundaries of the "situation" as it was defined, presenting a threat to the structure of the entire encounter (Goffman 1961). I had also expressly described myself as straight and a definite behaviour and vocabulary were expected from me. Consequently, I probably transgressed my personal boundaries when I once inadvertently used the words "blow job." The term elicited an embarrassed giggle from the informant, who might not have minded "frenching," but probably expected "oral sex" from a middle-aged and middle-class woman, or even "fellatio," if she knew the word. Respect for the established boundaries was often reflected in the informants' modesty. Most of them appeared careful not to say anything which might presumably shock me. What they thought might appear to me to be outlandish sexual practices, for instance, would be referred to as "something special." On the whole, they believed—and said so— that I was very conventional in sexual matters and would see as extraordinary what would be ordinary experiences for them. "Like, for you," said Jo, "something might be different, but for us, it's normal." When pressed— as, for instance, when trying to define for me the difference between *perverts, freaks, weirdos,* and *nuts*—Bugsy gave me examples but obviously did not enjoy doing so. By the same token, when I volunteered an example, always drawn from another informant's text, to confirm a definition, e.g. "If he wants to watch you pee in a glass, or if he wants you to pee on his face, that's harmless enough, but is he likely to turn dangerous as well and try to hurt you?" it was sometimes received with what appeared to be some embarrassment.

In a story related by Bugsy, her old man asked: "What were we doing?" when she told him that she had seen him with another woman. For my benefit, she explained: "So I told him! I described it right down to a tee!" the single exception to the otherwise verbatim retelling of the whole dialogue that had taken place during their quarrel. Another time, she related in some detail an encounter with a sailor, skipping over this passage: "I picked him up as a trick. We went to my girl friend's house and we did our thing." In the same manner, Julie said, "You pick up a trick and you go to his hotel room, and during the course of whatever may be happening or, turning out…" Her use of euphemisms was such that she often confused me entirely and, to spare her in her efforts to spare me, I preferred not to ask for further clarification. A possible explanation of this modesty may be found in Brandy's statement, "If someone gives me fifty bucks, I lose all modesty. But if someone's not giving me shit, I'm really modest."

I believed at the time that their frequent diffidence to discuss explicitly their sexual transactions with me was simply due to the fact that those very transactions constituted the main difference between us. What I came later to wonder was whether their discomfort was not mostly due to my apparent disregard for their discretion and my possible repositioning myself among the usual judgemental straight women. They may well have thought the questions *ignorant* given the context of courtesy and equality we had previously established.

Their respective sexual behaviour is naturally enough a topic of confrontation between straight and street women. In her introduction to *The Prostitution Papers,* Millett describes some shrill and discordant arguments between feminists and prostitutes, in the course of which was finally heard

> The accusation, so long buried in liberal good will or radical rhetoric ... The rejection and disapproval which the prostitutes have sensed from the beginning, and with the unerring instinct of the unconscious have directed all their energy toward exposing (Millett 1973:25).[5]

The cry: "You're selling it, I could too but I don't," in effect a triple statement, is all the more interesting then feminists are often the first to maintain that wives closely resemble prostitutes and buy with sexual favours or duties their husband's financial support and the security it brings, or that straight women repay men for the pleasure of being wined, dined, entertained, and flattered in the only way that is expected of them. Whereas this argument in the feminists' mouth is meant to stress the sexual and social subjection of all women, in the prostitutes' mouth it simply becomes a way to put down straight women and show

---

[5] "A hustler is any woman in American society. I was the kind of hustler who received money for favors granted rather than the type of hustler who carefully reads women's magazines and what is proper to give for each date depending on how much money her date or her tricks spends on her." (Terkel 1974:57)

that they have little reason to feel self righteous (since it is assumed they do) and superior to street women.[6] Understandably, when feminists do take up the argument, it is not well accepted by prostitutes. Or vice versa.

If some reluctance was usually shown when referring to explicitly sexual—occupational in this context—matters, it must also be said that coarseness was sometimes used as a weapon (defensive, retaliatory, or aggressive, depending on the interview situation). It was at least experienced as such, and while I accepted the customary street put down of the "ignorant" straight as a generalized antagonistic gesture, I apprehended the voluntary coarse sexual remark or suggestion as a personal affront. In fact, both were equally directed at challenging a straight woman's self perception as a liberal and open minded person. The stereotypic description of the straight women's hang-ups (served to make any personal reference a hostile challenge and an attempt to force the issue, very much as in the passage described by Kate Millett. But it is possible that this challenge was only a response to what may have been seen as an unfair excursion outside the parameters of the interview situation as they had been defined. On the whole, however, by never proffering any so-called liberal good will or radical rhetoric to my informants, I spared us both the embarrassment of their having to "set me straight." When our respective, yet similar, positions had to be discussed, it was often done tactfully and somewhat ironically.

In the following extract, for instance, Brandy switched around a popular statement: She did not say: "All wives are prostitutes." She said: "All husbands are tricks"; furthermore, when she compared us and said that we acted in similar ways and manipulated our men in identical fashion, she did not compare us as prostitute and straight woman, but simply as

---

[6] As Bugsy explains, "It was mainly a sex problem between them. 'The same old thing all the time!' that's what Joe said. He said he couldn't handle it. He said she refused to do it in a different way, because she did not know how. She was scared. She always had the Mommy image in her head: 'Don't do that! That's a naughty girl!'"

women: She spoke as an "old lady" (rather than as a prostitute) to a wife:

> You look through the centuries, they say the woman's been tied to housework and raising kids. But she's also-manipulated that guy to go out and slave his ass, bring home the pay check, feed her, take her out, wine, and dine her. And I think that now women are caught in their own trap. They manipulate a little too good! Because I talked to a lot of people and they'll say: "But how can you turn a trick?" And I'll say: "You guys turn a trick every time you fuck your wives!" And they say: "We don't turn ..." And I says: "Yes, you do! You're buying the groceries for the week, you're clothing her. And if she's not in the mood to get fucked that night, you'll say: "Well, let's go to a party, dear.'" and you relax her with booze and give her a good time, and <u>then</u> you get her in bed. And so every man is a trick!" It's true! Women have manipulated men and now they're balking because they're stuck in the kitchen!
>
> You take a good looking woman or a good looking man, and they can get along anywhere. If they have anything on the ball, they use their looks to play on other people. I used to do it when I was younger. I was cute when I was a kid, so I would just pucker up and throw a few cute tears and I'd get what I want. When I got older I had a good shape, so all I'd have to do is wiggle my ass past a guy and I got what I wanted, you know. Or, if your husband's horny, and you want a coat or something, you're gonna be as *nice* as you can, until you get that coat. And then you'll go back into your rollers and no make-up. And you want something else, so out come the rollers and on comes the make-up! I've done it all my life, and all my girl friends do it. Maybe they don't realize they're doing it, but they're doing it ... *You* probably done it!

If boundaries were usually maintained, they were also transgressed, and there was often an implication of female complicity during our interviews. It was more or less implied that, whereas the Street Trickster was beyond my experience, I would definitely guess what the Female Trickster was up to, and would know where and when to laugh. I rather doubt that a male researcher would have received exactly the same data. After our reciprocally tentative gestures of the beginning had finally gelled into familiarity, what they told me because I was a woman, they would have spared him because he was a man, unless they had meant to shock him out of his complacency. Even if the words had been the same, the intonation and the grins would have been different. And if those had been there, then the message they carried would have been different. To borrow Geerts' warning (1973:15-16), our *fictio* would have differed and our understanding would not have been the same.

THE DATA

The work done with the informants fell basically into three categories: elicitation of definitions and descriptions through questions and answers; collection of spontaneous anecdotes; and taxonomic classification.

Some women were ill at ease and moody, although on the whole willing to talk; others were helpful and painstakingly informative; others again were friendly and vivacious speakers. A few of them went through all three states over the months of the research. The informants and I naturally adopted a form of communication best suited to their particular talents, the relationship we had formed, and their mood of the moment. Bugsy, for instance, who could ramble on from one story to another with good humour, a good sense of timing, and a sarcastic turn of mind, sat with glazed eyes when I asked her to sort out and classify cards: within a few minutes, her boredom had made the atmosphere of the room unbearable. Dee and Sugar, on the other hand, dutifully performed the tedious classification over a period of several sessions, often puzzling at what they discovered, and saying they had never "thought about it like that before." Julie, whose inquisitiveness was always evident, appeared equally interested in providing definitions and descriptions, speculating on the differences between the two cultures, and discussing the system of communication and exchange between their members.

To start the first interviews, when I did not yet know the personality of the informants, I asked them all to name and describe the people they saw on the street. As these were named and described, a rough classification already took place into *street people* (traffickers, users, hookers, etc.) and *square Johns* or *straight* (shoppers, tricks, etc.). As the groups were further subdivided (e.g. different types of tricks, hookers, users, etc. see Appendix B), more definitions followed, characteristics, and stereotypes were expressed, and relationships were defined.

Some informants never confined themselves to straight answers. In fact, it was the measure of Bugsy's tiredness when she did, and I would then put an end to the formal interview. She, and at least two others, regularly substituted an anecdote for a definition. If I asked a question on the possible type of relationship between a "good cop" and a street woman, for instance, or on the way to handle drunken tricks, and answer very often took the form of a story. I assume that they found difficult to answer my questions with generalizations amounting to an interpretation of the culture's environment. An anecdote, referring to one incident in which the question asked found one answer, established instead the informant's cultural competence and her ability to deal with a definite, concrete situation. To an abstract statement on relationships, she substituted a concrete statement on specific interactions. From the sum of these situations described at length and repeatedly through street gossip emerge the approved behavioural limits of the group.

A few informants appeared to feel uncomfortable with the interviewing format of questions and answers, perhaps because it resembled too much police interrogations or interviews with correctional staff. They were instead encouraged to talk freely of their experience on the street, of what they perceived to be occupational and personal problems, and how they attempt to˙ handle these, and they usually responded to this request by retelling stories depicting problematic situations and usually successful outcomes.

Whether obtained through one informant's usual anecdotal way of answering questions or while relating a particular tale, part of the data consists of a collection of stories. Some of these stories, through the sheer context of the street's usual means of livelihood and survival, and the informants' self-perception, are versions of Trickster tales, describing how the straight trick or mark, whose intent is to exploit street women, are in fact tricked (manipulated or robbed) by them. They also described how informants came, successfully or not, to terms with problems arising from the illegality of their activities as prostitutes and drug addicts when encountering members of the narcotics and morality squads. Always, they attempted to trick those out to trick them. Finally, they described how the women's good faith is sometimes deceived by the "bad" tricks who rob and beat them, and how they meet such a situation, a situation for which they are always prepared. While this first group of stories described the interaction, always of an exploitative nature, between members of the two cultures, other stories established some of the parameters of in-group interaction and describe appropriate behaviour and sanctions for transgressing its guidelines.

A linguistics analysis went along with the collection of stories. Words intuitively deemed to be significant, or explicitly said to be so by the informants themselves, were extracted from the texts and classified in two ways: *alphabetically,* with their definition and often ample illustration of usage in context: either ad hoc examples provided by the women as they defined the terms, or extracts from the stories illustrating specific meanings and appropriate contexts; and *taxonomically,* into domains such as "straights," "tricks," "hookers," "addicts," "cops," etc. This classification was done by the informants as they reviewed some 200 cards bearing the words of the glossary and sorted them into a semantic grouping that "made sense" to them. Further sorting took place within each category, as words were discussed and the terms were ordered along vertical dimensions of generalization and horizontal dimensions of discrimination. None of my informants had done this type of semantic analysis before, yet they proceeded with great assurance. Much like Spradley and Mann's cocktail waitresses (1975: 61-62), it appears that prostitutes and drug addicts who work on the street operate with several sets of categories: some serving as a basis for the formal structure of the setting in which they operate and others understandable only in terms of their specific social networks. In the folk taxonomy established by the informants, people are clearly identified by their behavioural attributes, and socialization partly takes the form of learning the categories, networks among them, and rules for operating within these networks.

The texts and the taxonomy both reflect the informants' emic values, and both cultures are described and evaluated in terms of street emics. These data deal with physical and environmental devices for adjusting to, coping with, and even attempting to get the better of problematic or dangerous situations. The definitions and story excerpts were anonymously available to the informants and their comments served as validity and reliability checks.

Their folklore is essentially of an oral nature, for evident reasons. The culture's artifacts, such as *rigs* for *fixing,* makeshift apparatus for tattooing in jail, containers to carry small quantities of heroin, etc. are, apart from the syringes themselves, easily available, easily disposable, and usually objects with another quite innocent function: a child's balloon, a broken tooth brush, a sewing needle, a bottle cap, a filter tip, or some cotton batting, a spoon. Their use shows a degree of ingenuity but, because of their need to be inconspicuous, as well as easily and anonymously discarded, they have not given rise to any type of art. Thus, with the exception of tattooing, only the verbal arts have developed in the culture: The performance of gossip, the oral display of status, joking and swearing, the transmission of common knowledge and practical experience, the verbal manipulation of tricks or marks, all of these serve to achieve means of personal and cultural survival and are a source of common and individual pride.

CHAPTER THREE

STREET TALK: *RAPPING, CONNING, BULLSHITTING*

Rapping, conning, and *bullshitting* are ways to talk. Speech acts serve many purposes: they are used to insult, intimidate, amuse, cajole, coerce, seduce, appraise, greet, subdue, or impress. As the interlocutors and the purposes vary, so do the manners of speech. The informants clearly indicated an awareness of the importance of verbal transactions and the belief that they could expertly control these.

A female prostitute drug addict on the street (a *hooker* and a *hype)* could in the course of a day talk to her old man or her pimp, her mark, her girl friends, other hookers, other junkies, her connection (trafficker), a rip off, cops on the beat, members of the morality squad posing as customers, *narcs,* her tricks. The tricks alone might include a *drunk,* a *talker,* a *masochist,* or a *weirdo,* all requiring a different type of verbal manipulation on her part. Her alertness, her ability to evaluate people and their needs as well as their expectations of her, her anticipation of situations and their outcome, and generally speaking her precise understanding of her environment and the part she plays in it shape her style of communication.

The women I met all lived, lawfully or unlawfully, by their wits: shoplifting and the perhaps slightly more "professional" boosting, rehashing,[7] Welfare,[8] prostitution, robbing tricks, living off a mark (described by Jo as a combination of "conning" and "hooking"), B&E,[9]

---

[7] "That's when you go to the shop and shoplift something, right? You go back and you make like you've lost the price tag. And you get the refund, the money instead." (Jo)
[8] Dee once joked that the day the Welfare cheque comes in is "the hooker's day off."
[9] Breaking and Entering (article 306 of the *Canadian Criminal Code).* This offence used to be a typically male one, but female addicts now practise it frequently.

forgery, writing bad cheques (also known as *paper hanging* or *kiting),* or the occasional waitressing, described by Brandy as being a "good stall." Whatever the means of livelihood, the women make sure that these are turned to their greatest advantage. Talking a trick out of sex, for instance, is more advantageous than going to bed with him. If he can also be talked into giving even more money for the same lack of services, all the better. If, on the same basis, he can be turned into a profitable mark, this is a real success.

READING AND CONNING THE MARK

All the women boasted of having, at one time or another, a mark. The little given to him in terms of companionship or sex, the amount received from him (rented apartment, clothes, money, car) are all topics of conversation where the women's talent at conning is appraised and enjoyed. In jail, a mark's letters are shown to friends, and his visits are talked about. The faithfulness of marks is legendary and much to the women's credit: it is proof of their conning ability and a sign of their success in life.

In this chapter, I do not make any distinction between a woman's mark and a con artist's mark. The technique used for "reading" a mark is reputed to be the same in both cases, and the characteristics of both marks are also the same, as we will later see. From a straight point of view, they may appear to be two different people but, from the street, a mark is a mark. He or she is also a perfect "straight man" in the oral performance enacted, giving the expected cues to which the artist will reply with a display of verbal mastery. Snow, asked in what area of street activities she felt to be an expert, answered "Manoeuvring people into a position to give me money." And Jo added, "Speech. Being able to talk." Reflecting upon the qualities that make a good con artist, Julie explained that "75 per cent, I'd say, are good talkers. Conning, you more or less have to talk a lot, and you have to set an impression on the person."

I personally experienced this ability to "set an impression on the person," which all my informants believe they possess and which is an essential part of con artistry. It goes with the ability to elicit from the researcher interviewing them, who is in this instance assimilated to a mark, the nature of his or her needs in order to satisfy these in the informants' own way. Bruce Jackson noticed the evolution of his interviewing technique with his informants, petty criminals, addicts, and prostitutes, seeing in it an achievement of competence on his part. He describes the customary loss of sensitivity and gain of expertise which causes the researcher to stop conversing with people and start interviewing informants, but he also describes a type of informant's apparent cooperation which resembles the manipulative technique applied to marks.

> While working on these manuscripts I noticed some differences in my own techniques over the years. In the early tapes ... I seemed to talk a lot. I occasionally gave opinions. These were often more conversations than interviews ... I learned along the way that the questions you ask structure the statements you get, not only in form but in content and focus, so I decided to ask as few questions as possible and to make those as general as possible so the speaker could decide what he considered important enough to talk about. That is necessary if you want to get what he thinks important rather than what he thinks you think is important (Jackson 1974: 9-10).

In the following dialogue, where my questions are in italics, Dee describes this technique:

> - It's all his personality. You work on his weaknesses. Somebody who likes... Who's always wanted a daughter or whatever.. And that's a weakness with him. So, you let him more or less take care of you.
> - *Will you try to change your ways just to be like a daughter?*
> - No. You just work on that part of him and make him think of you as his daughter.
> - *Will you call him special names?*

- No. It never comes out right in the open, what you are doing, because it makes him self-conscious. You just work your way around him to get it.
- *So you have to try different approaches before you know…*
- Before you know which one is gonna work!
- *How much time do you have to feel that he could become a mark? Is it something that you can decide at once?*
- At once. You know whether he is. After sitting and having a drink with him or something… You just get to know their personalities. Like, some personalities can be marked in a lot easier than others. You listen to him talk and you get to know what he wants. And then, that's what you work on. His weaknesses.

Jo and Snow added a few precisions to Dee's description of the method:

- *What sort of "talking talent" do you have to have?*
- Manipulation.
  - Yeah. Put yourself to the level that you know they want to be and that they are.
  - Yeah.
  - *Which means that you have to listen too?*
  - Oh, yeah! You go by ear, you know.
  - *You listen first and you talk afterwards?*
  - Well, you start out slow.
  - Yeah. They're talking to you and you're answering them. Not giving yourself away by the answers. More or less that you're going along themselves, making them think, you know…
  - Until you have enough to go on that you know what they want.

Vincent Swaggi, Klockars' professional fence, would agree with these informants. From childhood, he says, "hustling taught me how to read people. I was as great bullshitter, a good con. I could tell nine times out of ten who I could sell. (Klockars 1974:38) Two of Blum's informants stress the dual and complementary aspect of information seeking and self-revelation:

> There's a con for every man. I'll just approach anyone and it will take me just fifteen minutes to learn his interests and his weaknesses ... The natural thing is to let the mark show you what he wants and then you just go along. (Blum 1972:30)

Con men often delight in describing successful "jobs." I could draw many illustrations of their skill from the literature or from my informants' text. I thought it more interesting and less customary to give a mark's version of such an experience. Reading con men's descriptions of their exploits, one may wonder how the whole transaction is viewed from the victim's standpoint and to what extent he is entirely fooled. The story in Appendix F was related to me by a friend, with embarrassment on his part and gratitude on mine. He describes how he became the victim of the "hot T.V. game." Reading the story, the advice of Klockars' informant may be remembered: "So you come over to him and you're looking around like there might be cops watching" (1974:43), which serves to confirm the authenticity of the deal by implying that the merchandise is indeed "hot." Interestingly enough in this case, the mark was actually prepared for a con job, but entirely misjudged its nature.

Street people believe they do possess a superior intuition, the insight to assess people and situations and the power to manipulate them. Writers who have worked with con men agree with this self-evaluation: "When it comes to "playing con" few people can match the skill and versatility of a "righteous dope fiend." (Sutter 1966: 211)

Michael Agar (1973:46) sees his confidence men, whether junkies or not, as "Good intuitive psychologists with poise and a sense of authority. They must correctly 'read' the *mark* and immediately formulate a strategy to encourage his trust." Maurer (1940:1-2) mentions "their high intelligence, their solid organization" their "superb sense of human nature." Con artists seem to have been endowed with or to have acquired almost superhuman qualities. Such a perfect match between a group's self image and the researcher's perception of the group leaves me a little uncomfortable, especially since the self-professed talent of that group is "to set an impression on the person," as Julie put it.

My occasionally inarticulate informants also claimed great intuitive powers and said that they *knew*. The field covered by that knowledge is almost limitless: they "know" what a trick wants just by looking at him, by extension what any man wants, and by a further extension, what any square John wants. Questioned further, they answered: "I just *feel* it!" Brandy explained that she *knew* how to "read" men and, at a glance, could tell what they wanted and how to adapt her own behaviour to deal with their anticipations, but she could not put that experience and that intuition into words. I suggested to her one particular type of man approaching in the street. "He is obviously ugly or repulsive or crippled or has something physically wrong with him, and presumably, going out with a working girl is the only way he can get it. What do you do?" "Well, they're self-conscious, so you're kinder to them to build their self-confidence. They're usually pretty straight and meek." Several women appeared to concur with this: Since greed and/or stupidity - the square John's trademark - are not the reason for that particular trick's request, they appear to be prepared to deal fairly with him. From Brandy, I elicited other impressions: "A good looking, well dressed guy: more kinky!" The apparent interpretation here is that, since he can "get it" elsewhere, he will obviously require special services. Old men are usually "perverted dirty old bastards." "The guys in taxis are the best: They pay the cabbies to find a girl." "If they're driving a Lincoln, they're cheap, they don't want to spent money: The money goes for the car!" "If they're driving beat up cars, they're more generous." The "Lincoln drivers," described by Brandy, were recognized with amusement by Bugsy and Julie as true to form.

Since it may be assumed that streetwalkers have gained some familiarity with physically handicapped, unattractive, or older men, as well as men cruising the streets in a taxicab looking for "a good time," they may have arrived at their definition of such types from solid experience. But the Lincoln drivers are somewhat puzzling. Bugsy and Julie's amused recognition stressed the unusual aspect of this type of customer and may lead one to wonder whether definitions may not result from striking but almost isolated occurrences as much as from a lengthy repetition of similar encounters. Whatever the basis on which they rest, stereotypes obviously contribute handy guidelines for the proper handling of people categorized as having these characteristics.

From the reading of such "clues" as described by Brandy, the informants appear to draw the guidelines of their occupational behaviour. For instance, in his first encounter with a prostitute when he first became a trick, G.L. Stewart (1972:270-271) simply described a competent operator, a woman who knew her job and could "read" a customer, and whose performance may be implicitly compared to that of a mechanic judging the problem by listening to a car engine, or a veterinarian the condition of an animal from the way it hangs its head: simple occupational experience.

> What had I given her to respond to, other than passivity
> and nervousness? Toward the nervousness she had
> directed behaviour intended to calm and relax me, and to
> the passivity she had responded logically and efficiently
> ("Just lie there and get raped"), perhaps even assuming
> that sexual passivity and surrender were my "thing." She
> had made the most of the clues I had given her.

Reading the mark is a skill sometimes acknowledged by the mark himself. It may be that stressing the con artist's talent at deception is a mark's way of reducing the part played by his own gullibility, once he becomes aware of the situation. He may be encouraged to do so by the con man himself to facilitate his recovery and the preservation of his self-image (Goffman 1952). The con man's guile is seen by both parties as complementing the mark's gullibility. But behind the mark's back, the con artist is likely to point out the former's greed, which it is his acknowledged talent to identify and bait appropriately. Some of the con jobs described in the literature are cleverly engineered and convincingly carried out. But even the seemingly rougher, coarser rackets of my informants appear to succeed. The reason for their success is claimed to be due to the victim's ignorance, stupidity, or greed. Such a characterization of the square John at large as ignorant, stupid, and/or greedy is indeed the one elaborated by street people on the basis of what they perceive to be the characteristics of individual straight people with whom they interact for their mutual exploitation.

Researchers in no way escape the stereotype, and informants transform the interviewers' needs into their own codes. In some cases, the interviewers' difficulties are compounded by the informants' added resentment at being in jail or under correctional supervision. By eliciting from them, whether they are social workers, psychologists, parole officers, probation officers—or anthropologists whose real powers are unknown—an indication of their intentions and goals, and providing the necessary responses to fulfill these, the inmates-con artists-informants test their talents at deception and control and, presumably, draw professional legitimization from the exercise.

James (1977:190) quotes from Maruyama on some of the problems of prison research where inmates feel exploited by the interviewers and attempt to minimize the exploiters' intrusion by using "sophisticated phony answers which make the interviewers happy." It would be simplistic however to view the interview as some interaction between seemingly cooperative but wily informants and naively happy interviewers. Indeed, the researchers' weariness of the informants' verbal skills is often expressed. They know that, when enquiring into verbal skills, they are faced with the danger that their practitioners may feel challenged to exercise them and that a competent performance on their part may cause the researchers to "buy" it. Jennifer James, for instance, in her work with prostitutes, is well aware of the problem. In the introduction to an unpublished report, she writes:

The informants know the researcher's world and deal with questions accordingly. With prostitutes this problem is compounded by the nature of the "hustling" business. For example, a prostitute depends for her success and survival on her ability to judge people and handle them - her ability to give the customer what he wants while not doing more than she wants. The prostitute is thus selling her ability to make the man feel he is satisfied. "Conning" is an art of the profession and the researcher is as likely a victim as the customer (James 1971:4).

As James points out, theses communicational skills are essential for the prostitute's survival. In a social interactional analysis of the folklore of a Texas Madam, Davis Johnson stresses the importance of her informants' feeling that "their most important work is mental and verbal—to remain in control of themselves and their interactions with the customers" (1973:219).

I cannot emphasize too much the importance of words in her life. Both she and the girls told us that the prostitute's art is much more mental and verbal than sexual. Men are physically stronger; therefore, to maintain constant control a prostitute must use words effectively ... (She) controls her environment through verbal manipulations (1973:212).

STYLISTIC DEVICES

As skilled verbal performers, my informants resort to many stylistic devices to render speech acts more effective. One, which is well illustrated in the Stories related in Appendix D, is the exaggeration of details, to catch the listeners' attention, strike their imagination, and perhaps serve to convince them faster—although, in many cases, the narrators simply seem to be carried away by sheer artistry.

Bugsy, for instance, is somewhat given to practice the well-known story telling device of magnifying incidents. In her case, numbers increase dramatically.

> I fixed 3 caps and I had a 8 narc escort home! She sent 8 cops out looking for me!

> The next thing I knew, there was 6 narc bulls and 4 policemen down there, looking for me!

> So, on the way up, I see there's 2 cop cars in front of us, 2 behind us, and I'm under arrest for soliciting!

Bugsy is a Granville Street hooker and a small time trafficker. I know, she knows I know, I know she knows I know that 8 cops, 6 narc bulls, and 4 policemen, or 4 cop cars would definitely not be mobilized to look for her. But she is also telling a good story to an appreciative audience, a story with a good plot and lots of action, obviously calling for Homeric proportions, and we are both to understand her figures as an artistic device used to establish her prestige.

In many instances, status is established by demonstrating how "bad" you are. The term is used in much the same way as in black speech where it expresses all the qualities of daring, cool, self-assertion, and non-conformity denied to the Negro defined as "good" by white society (Milner 1972a; Milner 1972b: 114). The prestige conferred by such statements is obvious:

> I'm barred from Newfoundland for life, because I pulled a bank robbery there. And they told me they were doing their federal prisoners a favour and send we back where I

came from ... They didn't want me to corrupt their prisoners! (Dee)

At one trial, they used my record as exhibit A! (Julie)

My record? The last five-six years, there's been mostly drug offences. And there's been robbery with intent to kill. I beat that. And a murder that I beat. (Dee)

A stylistic device employed to make a point clear while not stressing it in an obvious manner is the aside. I had to train myself to recognize it and its importance for my understanding of the context. For instance, Jo explained to Snow and me: "He was going to give me 200 dollars for one hour. That was up North". This last remark appears irrelevant to the story she was telling. Yet, the explanation was needed since, in Vancouver, girls like Jo and Snow are not paid 200 dollars for one hour of their time. But, up North, this could very well be true. I might not have been knowledgeable about the going rates but, since Snow was also present, the explanation provided in an aside was quite necessary to establish Jo's credibility. Had we felt, Snow in particular, doubts at this point, we might not have believed the rest of the story.

In the same interview, Snow explained: "I was arrested because I went and robbed somebody. Somebody I know!" Small time con artists usually practice a hit and run method. So do thieves. Robbing somebody is not dumb but—her intonation implied in the aside—robbing somebody you know and who knows you (especially, in her case, her mark) and is in a position to press charges, is *very* dumb! To give a last example, here is a story told by Bugsy:

I had this little ol' man, once. And this was cute ... He took me out. He paid me just for a straight, and his time was up and he hadn't even got it hard. And he wasn't drunk, he had nothing to drink. And he says: "Oh, dear!" he says, "my time's up!" Like, it was him that kept the time! I wasn't even lookin' ...

Bugsy's positive and even protective feelings towards her trick was expressed here in several ways: She calls him a "little of man" instead of the customary "dirty old man"; she describes the whole incident as "cute"; he paid her "just for a straight," i.e. he was not a weirdo, a freak, or a pervert; the disarmingly quaint "Oh, dear!" he lets out, while her usual exclamation is "Oh, shit!" or "Oh, fuck!"; his failing was not due to alcohol—drunks can be "flippy" (unpredictable) and take forever to perform, to the irritation of most prostitutes; but the greatest proof she gave of her good mood is that it was he and not she who "kept the time," whereas she would normally have said "Time's up!" at the end of the twenty minutes he had paid for (if not earlier, since he obviously was not going to finish before that time). The little aside was used to express most decisively her approval of the little of man and his sense of propriety.

I had expected in this essentially oral culture numerous formulae to anchor the speech and set statements into a context of popular tradition and consensus. Indeed, Sue sometimes punctuated an edifying story with "If you can't pay, you shouldn't play," and its echo "If you can't do the time, you shouldn't do the crime." Other women also mentioned that "Money's money" and "Time's money." But I found the use of pseudo-aphorisms, mock riddles, and individual definitions more interesting. There were also few of these, but they added spice to the story and stressed individual creativity in the performance of verbal skills.

- Welfare is the hooker's day off. (Dee)
- The good junkie is self sufficient. (Dee)
- How can you tell a junkie? By how much sugar she puts in her coffee! (Bugsy)
- How do you knot the narcs? When the door comes down! (Bugsy)
- You want a little love for a little money. I want a little money for a little love. (Julie)

There are not enough data available to analyze personal styles, but the examples taken from Sue, Dee, and Bugsy would seem to indicate a respective predilection for the proverb, the aphorism, and the pseudo riddle.

The delivery itself and speech habits are characteristic: the informants frequently intersperse "like ..." "you know," and use them to leave a sentence suspended or to force the interlocutor to make the necessary effort to meet them half way; or "right?", "hey?" followed by a brief interrogative mimic which could be answered with a faint nod or a grunt, or any other sign that you are going along with what is being said. The necessary participation of the interlocutor is required and the elicitation of her approval de facto turns the monologue into a dialogue.

Another characteristic of the informants' speech is the reporting of past dialogues in direct style. Beside the conventional alternation of the "I says - he says" insertions, some informants will break up a reported sentence several times with "he says," "so, I says." This contributes to the creation of a vivid and lively style. It seemed a very good device for keeping the interest of the audience, even if it slows down somewhat the development of the story.

> I asked him. I says, "You were out with Pete's old lady?" He says, "No." I Says, "You're a fuckin' liar!" I says, "I was sittin' in the car next to you," I says, "I seen you.'" He says, "Well, what were we doing?" So, I told him! I described it right down to a tee! He says, "What were you going at the show?" I says, "My mark took me to the show. I got paid 400 dollars to go to the show!" He says, "Where's the money?" I says, "I spent it!" He says, "On what?" I says, "Junk." He says, "Oh, you did, did you?" I says, "Yeah!" He says, "I gotta go sick, I gues?" I says, "Well, go get your other slut there to buy you some!" I says, "If she can afford you, if she can afford to go to bed with you," I says, "surely she can afford to buy you a cap of junk! "He says, "Here we go!" So I says, "Fuckin' right,

here we go!" I says, "Now, if you don't mind, I'm busy.
Hit it!" (Bugsy)

It will be seen further on that Bugsy has also drawn here very neatly the list of reciprocal duties and rights of an " old man" and his "old lady." Such an exaggerated form is obviously idiosyncratic in her case, but Bugsy is also, and by far, the most entertaining of my informants. I found that her emphatic usage of a very common mannerism among all my respondents, and many people of similar background, only contributes to the vivacity of her style, even if one can only take a little of it at the time.

This speech form relied on a temporal distortion: "there and then" becomes "here and now." The past is telescoped into the present as the conversation is relived: "he said" becomes "he says." This reported dialogue form also gives an important diachronic perspective of the self. The reported dialogue between ego-then and alter-then is presented to the researcher by ego-now, who appears not only as a reporter but also as a commentator, thus in a diachronic quality. Even if the reported dialogue did not involve ego, her presence is assumed. As a literal reporter her presence is essential to both events—then and now—and to both interlocutors. Ego's creativity as a speaker is given its due since she is in control of all speeches: those of ego-then, ego-now, alter-then and the researcher drawn into the present dialogue by the interrogative mimic and the pressure to provide her agreement.

Since much of the data is in the form of stories, anecdotes, retelling of specific incidents, the mechanics of tale beginning and ending are easily observable. By far the most common way to start a story is "There's this (guy I know, friend of mine, cop up North, trick had a wife, etc.)". Often the story peters out, but for Bugsy and Julie, for instance, the phrase was as recognizable as "once upon a time," and I automatically started my tape recorder upon hearing it. Story ending, on the other hand, is much more elusive. Even Bugsy often found it difficult to conclude her tales and it was only exceptionally that she arrived at a "conventional" ending such as in a story about a trick's wife, where the trick and his wife live happily ever after thanks to Bugsy's good offices. Most of the time, however, the anecdotes ended abruptly. This may have been seen as a stylistic weakness specific to Bugsy, who sometimes sighed and added "Fuck ..." or "Shit ..." as a formal if unsatisfactory conclusion. This need of a comment of sorts was often caused by my silence. The following is an example of a more elaborate ending also elicited by my intentional failure to respond to the natural ending of the story, which was:

> As soon as you say you've got a cop for a friend, everybody figures you're a rat. So I told him, "Well, you keep your mouth shut, I'll keep mine shut." He says, "O.K. You got a deal!" I says, "Either I got a deal or you ain't got a friend!"

Obviously, the story could have ended there to everyone's satisfaction, but because of the lack of natural context (where stories may be topped at once, or at least commented upon) and my failure to react, she hesitated and went on in a completely irrelevant manner:

> He's nice ... He's tall ... He's dark and he's blond ... I had my hair bleached white when I knew him. He says "You look like one of those Amazons". "Ooooh, get off the pot!" I says, "I got white eyes, I ain't got pink eyes!" Shit ...

Finally, the ending of a story will sometimes become the beginning of a new one, retold or not:

> And I says, "You're lucky, you know, because," I says, "cos if I was Pete," I says, "You'd be long gone. Down at the end of the Bow River, and if you're ever lost in that, they'd never find you," I says, "It took them two and a half months to find my baby sister ..." That was at Christmas ... But that's another story. (Bugsy)

MANNERS OF SPEECH

We have seen that the recognized art of conning the mark consists of eliciting the indication of his desires and needs, then finding a satisfactory balance between the woman's reluctance to give and the mark's greed to take. We also saw earlier various conventions of speech designed to define status, give information, establish bona fides, produce acceptable exaggeration (and not the type of exaggeration that simply betrays a lack of culture competence, such as Julie's claim to be carrying a .38). All these serve to illustrate part of the culture's verbal skills.

Many categories of speech acts are recognized by the informants who attach distinctive features, such as form, content, intonation, appropriate settings and participants, to various terms referring to manners of expression. The following is not an exhaustive list of terms, but a sample of those most frequently used.

Bullshitting

There are two meanings attached to *bullshitting,* describing very different types of situations and purpose. The first usage of the term refers to an attempt at deception and is used in the same context as *conning.* This is the usage already met in Swaggi's claim that he was "a great bullshitter, a good con." The second meaning simply refers to the type of small talk encountered in many groups.

Photograph courtesy of Lincoln Clarkes
(Worldwide Green Eyes)

I asked Jo and Snow:

> - *When you meet someone you know, what do you talk about?*
> - Small talk.
> - "How're you doin'?, "Oh, fine," "Right," "pretty slow
> today, hey?", "Right." You kow.
> - "So and so got ripped off by…"
> - "Who know who's got good stuff?" "Oh, yeah? Is that right?,
> "Oh, yeah!"

- "I did some stuff the other day that was dynamite!"
- Street talk, you know.

I had misunderstood, at one point, the second meaning for the first one. They immediately corrected me, and their awkward explanation actually made sense:

- Oh, no ... Well, it's not ...It's *real!*
- It's not bullshitting. It's just .. Everyday's happening on the street ...
- Yes, just small talk ... Just bullshitting, you know

The nature and function of bullshitting will be examined more thoroughly in the next chapter.

Talking

Talking is seen by my informants as the hustle par excellence.

I get enough by talking that I didn't have to go on Welfare. (Snow)

I talk to Welfare pretty good! (Snow)

I like talking to these people. They're so naive, so when you lay something on them, they're shocked! (Julie)

I just talk to them. I sit there and I *talk!* (Jo)

I phoned him and I talked. Again I talked` So he went down to drop the charges ... I talked to him. Put on my act ... He said he'd drop the charges, you know. (Snow)

Naturally, it has other meanings. In the above examples, the women talk "to set an impression," as Julie put it. In the following one, Snow talks in order to *receive* an impression: "I'll talk for a few minutes in the street, you know, to sort of getting an idea, you know. Then, I'll go [with him]. Only then." *Talking* is a manipulative exercise through which the informants obtain or retain control of a situation. Whether in an exploratory or an assertive transaction, the interlocutors are seen as verbal opponents to be overcome.

Conning

Conning also involves talking. "Conning, you more or less have to talk a lot" (Julie). It may also infer a stronger determination to deceive than the one implied in straight talking. If speech is not always explicitly mentioned, it is nevertheless part of the whole performance.

> Conning people to think that you're gonna go to bed
> with them, knowing that they have money. (Jo)

> When I'm on the road, I have no intention of trying to
> con them out of money. (Snow)

> Some heavies are liars, they con other people. (Brandy)

> Similarly, "I'd hit him for some money" implies the use of a verbal
> request.

Rapping

Rapping may indicate a certain degree of closeness between the speakers as well as some seriousness in the topic, as opposed to bullshitting which often refers to a superficial exchange. Jo makes it clear in the following exchange that one usually raps to one's friends:

> There are only three people in this building that I really rap to, or sit down and talk to ... The rest, it's very casual. I rap to these people because they're more real. I know there's no trips and no bullshit.

Unlike people in the black ghetto (Kochman 1969), street people also use *rap with*. In the following example, "rap with" is used to describe what Kochman's informants would call "putting the make" (1969:27) in the context of "rapping to" a woman (Burling 1970:157):

> I'll always tell other girls, if I see him rapping with them, or something. You know, just anybody I'm I'll always rapping to, I'll say "Hey, I met a really weird guy tonight. If you happen to see him, don't go near him!" (Jo)

Teasing and Preaching
These two terms indicate a manner of speaking as well as a definite purpose. They are in fact self-explanatory, but Snow usually specifies the manner in which this teasing or preaching are done:

> And they'd come and play pool with us, you know, talk to us, laugh with us ... play pool, tease us ... or else we'd be at a table and he'd be teasing us, right? "I'm gonna beat you guys at pool!" "O.K., You're on!"

> He used to say to us "God! It's too bad! I wish you girls would straighten up your act, you know. You would be really nice girls if you wouldn't be so carefree, so crazy!" Yeah ... Always more or less preaching away "Why don't you guys smarten up?"

Snow, in these particular examples, uses the verbs as pseudo- adverbial phrases, i.e. he said teasingly, he said in a preaching manner. Snow is a sentimental woman who often thinks back on the good times when she was just a rough tomboy Indian girl in Prince Rupert and not the thief and junkie she has become downtown. She likes to linger on the "teasing" and "preaching" given to her by a good-natured local cop— and we should note that she does not call him a pig, or a bull, or a narc—who liked her and was concerned about her. So, not only does she "name" that way of speaking but she also confirms the name by a description which could be used as a definition. Other examples of preaching only referred to various speeches made by "do-gooders," and not always positively.

Hassling

Hassling also refers to a complex action performed as a speech act, accompanied by implicitly threatening behaviour. Since it is always practised by *assholes* who, by definition, abuse their power, its usage is thus reduced to specific situations (narc and junkie encounters, for instance):

> They always hassle you, you know: "Oh, yeah? What's these marks are? Don't give me that story!" (Snow)

> They give you a lot of hassle, telling you to get off the street. (Dee)

Hassling always takes place between people of uneven status, power, self-assurance, or need, since the object of the transaction is to intimidate the interlocutor into submission or the relinquishing of whatever the speaker wants from him.

Making Like, Playing Like

These are aspects of the *con* or the *talk*. Again, this refers to a complex situation where the speech act is not necessarily mentioned but is nevertheless implied:

> I said "Yes? Me?", you know, playing like I've never ... you know ... (Snow)

> You go to the store and shoplift something, right? You go back and you make like you've bought it, but you've lost the price tag. (Jo)

> I said, "I think I've got it". I know I had it, but I was playing, you know, like ... casual ... (Snow)

Once more, they are "setting an impression." The moves described here are relatively simple ones. When the situation becomes more complex, one may be "laying something" (a "trip," for instance) on someone: "They're so naive so when you lay something on them, they're shocked" (Julie).

A series of verbs indicate the embarrassing and hesitant context of prostitution and the manner in which information is sought and given:

> Sometimes, they try to *beat around the bush* to find out if you're a working girl, because he doesn't want to put himself in a position to *ask,* and you're not ... When you're walking along to the hotel, you sort of *drag out* what he'd like and you *discuss* it ... They usually *bring up the subject* of what they like. (Jo and Snow - *my emphasis)*

To *ask,* in this context, when done by a man, is short for "to ask a working girl to go out." When the woman "asks," it is usually followed by a dollar figure. Events such as *noticing, believing, stopping* (someone on the street), etc. when retold, can be immediately followed and without transition by direct speech: "All of a sudden, they notice you: 'Hey! Who's that?'" (Jo), "They believed me: 'Well, you be on your way!'" (Snow). This stylistic short cut, by naming the mental process of the speaker, reestablishes in fact the logical sequence of the steps which led to the spoken sentence quoted by the informants. The structure is naturally not peculiar to street people and simply reflects an awareness of the psychological context of various speech acts.

While, once again, none of the previous examples can be attributed only to those informants we call street people in this work, they all reflect the vivacity of style, the verbal skills, and emphasis on speech peculiar to a group who relies almost exclusively on oral means of communication and transmission of experience.

SWEARING

I cannot evaluate the incidence of swearing on the street, since I only dealt with women in jail. Many of the women who talked to me, however, mentioned that their vocabulary was much cruder and more violent in jail. Sue felt "dumb" when we went back out and started swearing as she did in jail, and Bugsy felt that "people looked" at her for the same reason. Jo disapprovingly explained that "swearing becomes a way of life in here." They assumed that the frustration of life in jail was the cause of their change of vocabulary.

Becker, analyzing the usage of "four letter words" notes that "the word takes on the immediacy of the act itself" and that

> Usually we use four letter words in situations where we have no control, where we feel vague and aimless - as in military life. Continual cursing seems to give us tangibility, decisiveness; it brings us back strongly into the world (Becker 1971:94-95).

When Coutts was a matron in the same prison (Oakalla), *The Manual* specified that "a girl is not allowed to swear in this institution" (Coutts 1961:75) and some matrons strongly believed that cutting out "street talk and filthy talk" was a sine qua non condition of rehabilitation and training (1961:91). If one of the functions of swearing is to bring one "back strongly into the world," as Becker writes, its prevention may presumably contribute to cut one off from a world deemed unsuitable. Although swearing is still discouraged in jail, it was not unusual for me to overhear from the office I occupied one inmate yell to another "If you go into my room one more time, I'll break your fucking arm and your fucking neck!" in tones that were deterrent enough.

The vocabulary lends itself well to cursing, swearing, and abusing people. Kontrowitz (1968), acting on the principle that what is important enough to be perceived is also named, found 184 names given by jail inmates to homosexuals, proving—if it needed proving again—the wealth of vocabulary of a deviant argot. My informants give names to a number of people possessing strongly negative characteristics: asshole, jerk, punk, prick, goof, pest, pervert, weirdo, nut, freak, flip, rip off, sadist, rat, pig, bull, etc. To these, I could only oppose, taken from all the texts: "she's good people," "he's a friend," "he's a good shit," and "they're solid." I found such a paucity of positive terms remarkable and I mentioned it to some of my informants who agreed with my examples and were themselves surprised. One suggestion made was that, in jail, they hated everyone and everything, and that this might very well be reflected in their vocabulary. Upon reflection, however, they could not add to my brief list of positive terms.

JOKING

As with swearing, I cannot evaluate the incidence of joking on the street. It was with Brandy, Tiny, and Sugar, who were housed separately in the Protective Custody section and who sometimes invited me for dinner that I had my first experience of jokes freely exchanged. They were mostly drug related and only became "jokes" as an afterthought, because drug is in everybody's mind. For instance, I was feeling the dirt around a potted plant and remarked that it was "pretty dry," forgetting a previous definition of "dry" as being "when there's no dope around." Tiny answered absentmindedly, "Yeah, everything is pretty dry around here," then,
actually hearing what she had said, laughed. Another time, Tiny mentioned that her jeans were too loose at the waist and she needed another pair. A member of the staff asked, "Why don't you fix them? You're pretty good with a needle," then realized the play on words and everybody laughed.

Greetings and brief exchanges between women who afterwards describe themselves as friends often take the form of insults. Abrahams, in his analysis of "black talk" on the street points out that apparent aggression is an essential part of joking activity or street play, and that for play to operate successfully,

There must be a recognizable relationship between it
and the real world. One of these vital connections is that
for play to operate successfully, there must be a sense
of threat arising from the 'real' and 'serious' world of
behavior. The threat of incursions from the real world
must be constant. That is, in the most successful kinds
of play, the most constant message must be the deeply
ambivalent one: this is play—this is not play. With
joking activity (which accounts for most playing in the
street world) this paradoxical message is very
commonly carried out by the use of the same
aggressive, hostile formulaic devices found in use in
real arguments—i.e. this is precisely what one finds in
the Black street world—so much so that the passerby
often has a hard time discerning whether joking or a
real argument is taking place (Abrahams 1974:245).

The following example provided by Brandy illustrate very well
Abrahams' point. She also indicates how carefully one must handle such
a situation.

I have this friend that's half Indian. I call her "Hey, you
fuckin' waggon burner!" and she calls me "Puerto Rican
cunt!" and people who see us together think we're
gonna fight. But we're friends and we know just how far
we can go.

Jokes are also used to relieve tension in problematic situations. In the
next example Brandy quotes a guard whom she considers to be a "real
gentleman" and describes a fight which had started playfully: She and
her friend knew "how far" they could go, as in the previous case, but
had just reached the critical limit:

She was holding me like that, see, and I was holding her.
She wouldn't let me go because she knew I would hit her,

> and I wouldn't let go because I knew she'd hit me. And
> we were going like that, and it wasn't funny anymore. So
> he says: "You guys want some music so you can dance?"
> Well, it was so funny that we broke up!

They broke up literally, because they broke up laughing first, as a face-saving device thoughtfully provided by the guard.

Another type of joke—often used by street people with members of the straight culture—is a direct challenge to the latter's assumed self-righteousness. It takes the form of a denial of having committed a reprehensible or unlawful action, giving as an alibi that you were, in fact, at the same time busy committing an equally reprehensible or unlawful action.

> Julie (relating an exchange between herself and a
> policeman), "Are you a user?" And I says- "Hell, no! I'm
> an alcoholic!"

> He couldn't have been trafficking when they said he did,
> because at that time he was passing bad cheques! (Julie)

> I wasn't soliciting when he busted me… In fact, I was on
> my way to score! (Bugsy)

The pause that followed, so brief as to be barely noticeable, was a cue to laughter, received with appreciation. I acknowledged the "naughtiness" of the remark and, presumably, appeared to condone the naughtiness of the intention. What I certainly did was to respond to an offer of complicity.

Coutts (1961:134) mentions the complicity into which matrons are sometimes drawn. With them the situation is naturally different; but, as a straight person, I was expected to feel uncomfortable at seeming to condone that of which I disapproved. However, once more, the "definition of the situation" and our relationship were such that I could not allow the joke to pass without acknowledging it. Moreover, I had also labeled myself an anthropologist, one for whom there was neither "right" nor "wrong" only what "worked" and what did not; and that, too, had to be tested.

The only joking behaviour I personally observed among inmates themselves took the form of one-liners and come-backs, which will be considered for their value as status markers in the next chapter.

ARGOT AND COMPETENCE

It is at once apparent that street people speak a language all their own, although, when speaking to square Johns street people use the latter's terms in order to be understood. My informants' general compliance and their usage of a common language make it at times easy to overlook the difference of terms. In the questions I asked Dee, my first informant, for instance, I used such terms as "heroin" and "night club." Dee answered with "heroin" and "club." In my notes, I reported "heroin" and "night club." One day, she used "policeman." I was surprised and asked, "Would you normally use the word 'policeman'?" "Only when talking to square Johns," she replied. "What other words do street people use when talking to square Johns? Do they ever say 'heroin' among themselves, for instance?" Naturally, I had to go over all my notes and check them. In the case of "night club," it was simply a case of inattention: Dee and all the other women only said "club," which is quite logical, since bicycle clubs, sports clubs, etc., are meaningless in their way of life and the only professionally relevant "club" is the "night club." They simply avoided what they saw as a redundant form, while I automatically imposed in my own vocabulary.

The acquisition of street language, made to appear difficult or beyond the comprehension of the average person, is the key to a prestigious insiders' world. Jo and I were talking about the type of conversation she and an ordinary square John like me could have if we met on the street corner in circumstances that would make conversation possible. She explained: "Well, you wouldn't use the same words as I would, talking to another person on the street. That would be a little different... Probably you would not catch the point..." Hence, the need for her to come to my level of ignorance in order to be understood. I once asked Snow if the straight people who spend a certain length of time working in arcades, pool rooms, beer parlours patronized by rounders and other street people, were not eventually able to understand them. She said doubtfully: "Oh, maybe things like "far out! ... But that's all." This was no doubt wishful thinking on her part, but the attitude reflects very likely the superiority felt by street people in having a different, commonly shared, and bonding language. Certain terms have seeped into the general language to facilitate professional and personal transactions between the two, groups (trick, mark, french, con, old man, pig, bull, etc.). These terms, a concession of sorts, are deemed to be so elementary that anyone who does not understand them—like Boots' "English duke," for instance—is thought to be "really stupid, or something." (see Appendix D)

An interesting point made by Polsky (1969) is that the special language developed by a socially deviant group is not devised, contrary to general belief, as the means of protection which secrecy would provide. At first glance, it would appear to do so because it has special terms for every process of the criminal activity concerned, and for distinguishing outsiders from insiders: It requires a competence not achieved by outsiders. But Polsky and Maurer (1940), the only linguist Polsky credits with common sense on this point, recognize in these characteristics the mark of professional affiliation and probably no more. Halliday, however, sees as *argots* those languages whose features are "no more than the technical and semi-technical features of a special register," but names *anti-languages* (i.e. languages of anti-societies) "the professional jargons associated with the activities of a criminal counterculture." (Halliday 1976: 571)

This so-called secret language is in fact relatively easy to acquire and not quite the profound expression of a hidden worldview. Policemen know it. Lawyers and judges, dealing with petty crime, know it. Some social scientists make it their field of study, and other rounders, very likely know it too. So, why the pretence that it is singularly intrinsic to the culture, and what purpose does it serve? Polsky and Maurer's main argument against the validity of seeing a protective device in criminal argot is that it is used by the speakers only when among themselves, when secrecy from outsiders is not required (Polsky 1969:99), since its usage when among outsiders would immediately label its speakers as deviants (Maurer 1940:284). Halliday (1976:572) quotes a study on Calcutta underworld where the question of why what he calls "anti-languages" are used was asked of 400 "criminals and anti-social elements." Of the respondents, 158 explained it as "the need for secrecy," apparently agreeing with the common belief. More interestingly, 132 saw its use as "a communicative force or verbal art."

I do not believe that this special language of theirs offers the small- time criminals from whose group my informants are drawn any protection against the police. The square Johns are not affected by it since they seldom have access to it. What are the need for and the function of such a language, then? Polsky believes quite simply that this type of argot

> Develops partly to provide a shorthand way of referring
> to technical processes but partly also as an elaborately
> inventive, ritualistic, often rather playful way of
> reinforcing group identity or "we feeling." (1969:99)

Maurer also explains the needs for this common language:

> Criminal groups or *mobs* work outside the law and
> consequently count very little upon it for protection.
> There is a very strong sense of camaraderie among

criminals, a highly developed group-solidarity, which is further increased by internal "organization" and by external pressures from both the upper world and the predatory underworld. A common language helps to bind these groups together and gives expression to the strong fraternal spirit which prevails among them. This is true of the entire underworld, with the partial exception of prostitutes. On the other hand, each specific trade or profession develops a feeling of mutual exclusiveness among its members; this feeling springs from 1.he fact that they are all criminals, that they have a commonality of life-experience, that their training and background are somewhat similar, that they face identical mechanical problems which must be solved with somewhat similar tools and techniques, and that certain professional attitudes or "ethics" must be recognized if the mob is to prosper (1940:283-284).

Maurer's reference to the prostitutes is rather ambiguous. Does he mean that prostitutes are exceptional (even partially) because they do not have a common language; because this common language, if they have one, does not help bind them as a group; or because they do not share a strong fraternal feeling? As it turns out, he means all three in a previous article (1939) and gives the following reasons for the lack of argot he found among prostitutes: "They lack the sophistication to make and acquire an artificial language for themselves" (p. 546); "She never develops a sense of trade, or group solidarity, of gang morale" (p. 547); "The prostitute sells a standard service and depends heavily on simple commercial good-will ... There is neither incentive toward a classification of her patrons nor a psychological approach based on such a classification" (p. 549).

There is a prostitute argot, however, and Jennifer James amply proves it (1972a; 1972b; 1972c). She also insists in all her work on the strength of the commitment that prostitutes have to make to the "fast life" because of the moral and legal sanctions inflicted on them by the larger community. She is also clear on the part played by a common language:

> Acceptance in the prostitute social organization depends to a great extent on the ability to communicate in the argot. The newcomer learns the rules as she plays the game ... If she handles her game well and can communicate in the acceptable manner, she can function as a member of the social organization. (1972b:103)

Unlike Maurer, James also describes a fairly supportive milieu where the prostitute always knows some people willing to offer her shelter, bail her out of jail, and welcome her if she decides to move away or leave her pimp (1972b:104).

Maurer sees the prostitutes' lot essentially as a passive one. It stands to reason, however, that if the streetwalker wants to survive she has to handle various situations in the context of her occupation, and has been led to name and classify a variety of customers. James' informants recognize fifteen different types of tricks, four of them "freaks." Mine also gave me fifteen different types of tricks, grouped into those "it's all right to go out with" and "those you should stay away from." (see Chapter Six and Appendix B).

Maurer writes that "the argot vocabulary which applies strictly to the profession appears to consist of less than fifty words." (1939:546) In her dissertation, however, James collected over two hundred terms which she classified into four domains (streetwalkers, tricks, pimps, and "stable sisters"). Maurer's arguments may have been valid in the late 1930s, at the time of writing. The prostitutes he describes had the choice of three possible set ups: living in a brothel, working in a "call-house," or "working the street." In the streets, they were "perpetually on the defensive... (and) never permitted to develop professional independence, which appears to be the first essential in the formation of criminal argots." (1939:547) The low status of prostitution in the criminal world denies them "all claim to true professional status." Moreover, he

92

continues, police oppression and the tightening of the bonds which ensues, are also missing from the prostitutes' life.

Between Maurer and James, more than thirty years have elapsed. If we look at the more recent terms elicited by James, especially in the domains of the pimp and the "stable sisters" (women working for the same pimp), we see the very strong influence of black jargon. Iceberg Slim's *Pimp. The Story of My Life* (1969), known by pimps and hookers as *The Book,* and Milner & Milner (1972) make abundantly clear the influence of black American pimps - whose style and prestige have earned them much prestige - over the conduct and language of prostitution. My Canadian informants, who usually deny that they use such terms themselves, know them nevertheless and characterize them: "That's nigger talk," "The black guys call it like that." In James, we see the enrichment of prostitute argot partly due to the control exercised by a group with a thriving and colourful language of its own.

The growing visibility of street prostitution has also increased police interference and control and, by the same token, the tightening of the streetwalkers' ranks, creating the need for a common insiders' language. The desire of prostitutes to professionalize their occupation has given rise to such organizations as the West Coast COYOTE (Call Off Your Old Tired Ethics) or the British PUSSI (Prostitutes United for Social and Sexual Integration), not to mention the French prostitutes' strike of Summer 1975.

In the case of my own informants, there is an added factor, one which differentiates them from James' streetwalkers and further links them to an "insiders' group": although sharing the technical skills of prostitution and the problems the occupation entails, my informants are also drug addicts, and James' were not. Hers were deliberately chosen as such in the Seattle jail. The same choice would have been impossible for me in the British Columbia Provincial Jail, since the inmates who were also prostitutes were, first and foremost, junkies.[10] Their argot is that of the

---

[10] This was specially true at the time the research was conducted (mid-1970s). The police were waiting for a Supreme Court appeal before making further arrests, and simple soliciting charges were

junkie, as well as the prostitute. Their lifestyle is that of the junkie as well as the prostitute. Prostitutes *score* when they turn a trick, junkies do it when they buy dope. Turning a trick, scoring, and fixing are the usual succession of events for the junkie-hooker; soliciting and scoring for the ordinary prostitute. The shift of meaning and emphasis of the success of the "score" from the non-addict to the addict streetwalker is revealing of the totally different outlook of the two types of women.

I also think that another relevant point is that the non addict prostitute only shares her argot with other prostitutes and with pimps (the two extremes in terms of occupational status and sex roles), making very clear her own position as the most inferior one, whereas the junkie-prostitute, who usually traffics, shares her argot with her equals, other junkies, males and females, among whom her own status is not dependent on sex or occupation, but on whether she happens to have heroin for sale. That particular argot introduces her into a basically equalitarian group and may be seen as more desirable than one that restricts her to a permanently lowly position. Moreover, a dealer is someone whose services are highly prized by street people, while a prostitute's are only appreciated, and very ambiguously at that, by her straight customers. The prestige of the former is by far the higher. And so is the argot of the subculture.

I found among my informants a sororal feeling, the tight bonds among members of the same group. However, this feeling exists because the women see themselves as street people, not as prostitutes. Towards non-addict prostitutes, their feelings are more reserved and quite ambivalent. This latter group is seen as "street" because of their common lifestyle and experience, but also as "straight" because of their values. The double dichotomy present-future and freedom-security, which will be discussed later and which polarizes "street" and "straight," also divides users and non-users among prostitutes.

---

not laid over a period of several months. Thus, prostitutes who were incarcerated at that time had been arrested and sentenced on a drug or robbery charge. Those with earlier soliciting charges would have already completed their term or were on the verge of being released.

All my informants expressed pride in and jealousy of their language. The following examples come from Julie:

> So, we're getting close to *where* I'm getting off, and he says "Well, would you like to do a trick?" And I says: *"Do* a trick?", I says, "don't you mean *turn* a trick?" And he says: "Oh, yeah! That's it! That's it!" And I says: "Do a trick ..." And I just laughed ... I mean, what kind of a trick did he want me to do?

> After I scored, I got back to him and I said "O.K., now you've got to get me a rig!" I don't know what he was thinking about ... "rig" ...He said: "Oh ...", he said "Ah ..." He was a truck driver, too. He said: "Oh, my rig's at ..." I says: "Hey! I'm sure you don't use heroin ... You just don't appear to be the type." So, he says: "What's this rig business?" So, I says: "Well, you have to go to a drugstore and get me an outfit, a syringe."[5] And he says: "Oh JEEEEZUS!"[11]

Whereas in the second example, Julie is merely amused by the play on words and the truck driver's lack of sophistication (shown by her own exaggerated use of straight terms), she openly sneers at the first man's attempt at talking like a rounder. Not only does he betray his ignorance of the argot, but he is despicable because he tries to pass himself off as a knowledgeable person. Moreover, the degrading implication of "doing a trick" is not lost on Julie, from whom "turning" one, on the other hand, is merely business. In this sense, he is *ignorant* in both languages.

The possession of a common language establishing the boundaries of a community and indicating membership in a common culture strengthens the bonds among group members and is valued because of it. In the present case, verbal skills are all the more valued that they are some of the culture's few non-violent weapons for exercizing control over both

---

11. By the mid-1970s, tighter conditions prevailed, compared to the situation described by Stoddart (1968:3-4), where a small enveloped containing "an inexpensive hypodermic needle, a syringe, and a bottle cap" could be obtained in a drugstore from the same area for 53 cents by asking for an "outfit" or a "machine" *[now called a "rig"]*, much as a few years later, kits of airplane glue and plastic bags were easily available from grocery stores.

insiders and outsiders.

CHAPTER FOUR

BULLSHITTING: NATURE AND FUNCTION

Bullshitting is the mainstay of street talk. It has already been examined in its two aspects: a con, a trip, a tall tale—and the small talk between people who share enough understanding of the same language and the same culture to converse in an easy manner. It is its dual or combined nature and its function that we are going to consider in relation to the informants' apprehension of their environment. Its limits are not easy to define since bullshitting is both *content* and *form*. We will see that beside its two manners of expression, it has two different goals: to *deceive* and to *instruct*. Although I did not witness either aspect of bullshitting being performed in the street context, a mild form of bullshitting was forever present in the exchanges which took place between my informants and me. In fact, it was the blending of its dual aspect which particularly interested me.

I found it difficult to organize my data into recognized folkloric genres, since as well as jests, jokes, trickster tales, proverbs, or aphorisms, so much of it was the repetition of hearsay and the passing of gossip. But gossip itself is a conversational genre, with its standard casual story-telling patterns and its following of some of the dictates of conversation such as the need to appear spontaneous. (Abrahams 1970:299)

THE NATURE OF BULLSHITTING

I found many similarities between my informants' casual bullshitting and the *talking trash* of Cothran's informants in the Okefenoke Swamp Rim of Georgia. Talking trash is described as ranging from small talk about the weather to discussion of the respective merits of brands of pickup trucks, interspersed with some teasing, joke telling, and yarn

98

spinning. It is defined as "loafing and lying behavior," comprising a variety of folkloric genres but unified in its context (Cothran 1974:342).

As small talk, what events does bullshitting cover on the street? Jo and Snow already gave an example of it in the previous chapter. Sue also described two other aspects of street gossip:

> Well, someone comes up from the street and says "I saw so and so, and they're doing really well!" (You know, they're staying off the drug and not using, or they're not drinking too much, or they're not taking pills, or whatever their weakness is, they're not indulging in it too often). You talk with just people you run into, acquaintances.

> People run stories about somebody else, you know. Mostly they talk about bad things. If it's something about a friend of yours, they can't wait to spread the bad news. Like, if they know your old man is going out with somebody else, they can't wait to tell you! You get it really bad in here *[jail],* more than on the street. You know, people like instigating, in here.

She also confirmed the range of circulation already mentioned to me by Julie, and the continuum between street and jail mentioned by all the informants:

> Stories spread like wild fire. They'll start in the street, and they'll be in here, and back in the street within a week ... usually with a little bit added here, a little bit added there ... Some time you'll even hear about them in Calgary or Edmonton, or back East, you know. I've heard a lot of stories about back East.

Jo had already indicated that warnings were an important part of street talk. This was confirmed by Sue:

Stories like that (about bad tricks), the girls tell themselves, warning people against the guy in case he's creeping around here ... You want to keep your distance from them. Or people selling bad dope, you know, you warn people about it.

Bugsy, in her inimitable style, gives other examples of bullshitting:

Sure travels fast! "Oh, did you know so and so robbed a trick last night?" or "Did you know so and so fucked so and so's old man?" Some pretty good things, too: "Hey, did you know Bugsy was on escape?" "Far out!"

Julie, who had a straight upbringing and is married with a child while very much belonging on the street, added yet another dimension to street talk:

You see each other, and there's a lot to talk about, and what's going on now ... You go back over what's been happening, and talk about, you know, a lot of things. And it's not just what's happening downtown that you talk about, because some people have met other people's families, and you know, being in the homes and have dealings with them; maybe growing up with them ... So it's not just going down there to talk about what's going around ...

In Julie's terms, a lot of things, *trips* and others, are being *laid* in these talks. Thus, one form of bullshitting blends with the other. Moreover, they were also often bullshitting me about bullshitting, an event within an event, and re-enacted the street-straight manipulative confrontation which forms the didactic content of many of the stories.

The stories told are obviously of a more elaborate nature than the dialogues reproduced for me by Jo, Snow or Bugsy. They are about an event (a bad trip, a freak you go out with, your old man going out with So and So's old lady, being hassled or busted). These narrated events, above and beyond the greetings and chit-chat which act as feelers for recognition and acknowledgement of inclusion, are the depository of the culture's wisdom.

Abrahams notes that in the black-speaking community, there are three basic types of street-talk events:

> Those intended primarily to pass on information, those
> in which interpersonal manipulation or argumentation
> involving a display or wits is going on, and those in
> which play is the primary component of the interaction
> (1974:246).

Although the last type of event is not developed here to the level of the verbal art form described by Abrahams (1974), Kochman (1970), and Milner & Milner (1972), all three are present and easily recognizable. I do not think that I was stretching the limits of the genre when I decided, for the purpose of this work, to include all talk. What was not good-humoured *inclusive* bullshitting was deceitful *exclusive* bullshitting. According to my definitions, my informants were either bullshitting with me or bullshitting me. In so doing, they practised in the latter what they preached in the former.

THE FUNCTION OF BULLSHITTING

The world emerging from the stories they told me is one of treachery and violence, where friends are few, even if acquaintances are many. With the latter, it is important to establish a tenuous network of small favours rendered and owed; of tricks, cop, and rip off warnings; and also of bullshitting. The favours and warnings are *prestations*, in the sense used by Mauss to signify things given in an apparently voluntary, disinterested, and spontaneous manner, while being in fact obligatory and interested. The economics and politics of street survival are indeed based on this system of prestations. Bullshitting is also part of the same system, since many of the things exchanged are "courtesies, entertainments, ritual" (Mauss 1969:2), to which bullshitting events would be assimilated.

> The disconnected small talk and the retelling of events, exchange of news, gossip of escape, busting, hassles, bad tricks and good marks, good "junk" and bad "shit," serve as an ongoing definition of the boundaries of the street community by constantly differentiating between straight outsiders and street insiders. By the same token, they provide convenient endo- and exo-stereotypes. They also serve as a means of socialization by redefining each time the rights, duties, and sanctions for transgressions for street performers, thus reaffirming the bonds among them. This is often done through personal-experience stories, the type of stories sometimes qualified as "lies" by the corrections officers, the type of stories where the interweaving of fact and fiction "proves so smooth than one could not separate the two strands even if it were important to do so" (Cothran 1974:346).

In the fine balance achieved in these stories between fact and fiction, the part played by each is difficult to assess. But fact and fiction are equally relevant, and one would have to go as far as Cothran, for whom

> What actually took place was decidedly less significant than what is alleged, imagined, or wished to have happened ... A fantasy is neither true nor false. Rather, it has a particular degree of experienced reality or unreality, as prescribed by society or by a deviant individual (Cothran 1974:343).

Bullshitting, like myths, fairy tales, or riddles, sets the coordinates of a relevant universe. The occupants of my informants' universe are divided into the Street and the Straight. Most people fit neatly into one group, while some loiter on the margin of one group with their affiliations or interests in the other. But, on the whole, the characteristics of the large cast of characters found in the tales are polarized into two contrasting groups, with opposite values, experience, and attributes. The two opposite groups are ideally represented. The Street, free and living in the present and for now, leading an exciting life full of thrills and fraught with danger, full of generosity and cleverness, and the Straight, sacrificing excitement for security in a doubtful future, living a life of drudgery and petty duties, full of greed and ignorance. In such a simplistic universe, one's allegiances are made clear and so is one's sense of duty.

If the experienced reality does not always correspond to the ideal representation, the lesson remains nevertheless. And the model is seen as true, even if it is recognized that some people do not conform to it, even if the non-user prostitute has straight values, if the straight fence is involved in criminal activities, and the street rip off is as greedy and stupid as the square John. The exceptions reinforce the rule, since they are indeed perceived as exceptions. In some cases, they are also named: *acey-duceys* with "a foot in and a foot out."

As in most societies, a sense of temporal and cultural continuity is provided by the reminiscences of long time participants in the culture. Comparisons between *then* and *now* oscillate between the poles of the "good old days" and the "it was tougher then" positions. Stoddart's informants (1968:89), a decade earlier than mine, already looked back upon an undeniably less strict era. Since the function of the statements is to enlighten the uninitiated observer, explicit comparison is made with contemporary conditions.

None of my own informants would have known the situation described by Stoddart above, the Golden Age of drug addiction in Vancouver, as it were. They look back upon times when the confrontations between drug addicts and drug control officers were physically more violent, and "old timers" such as Brandy and Sue recall occasions where people, and often themselves, were "throttled," "choked," and "punched." When a comparison with present times is explicitly provided, "hassling" in its many forms is mentioned and one does not get the impression that the situation has necessarily improved. In every case, the description of the hostile forces at work serve to strengthen group solidarity.

The diachronic, historic perspective is complemented by tales of elsewhere, in which *there* is compared with *here*. Both Stoddart's informants (1968:89) and mine agreed that (a) elsewhere is different, and (b) local residents are in the less enviable position, usually because of law enforcement policies and methods. Spatial continuity is thus also provided, and both dimensions serve to affirm the concept of a drug addict community expanding beyond the immediate confines of the present and one's *Corner*.

The historic and geographic evaluation of the nature and quality of the street addict's environment is all the more important that there is no formal apprenticeship on the street. Unlike criminal occupations practised off the street (Letkemann 1973, Bryan 1965), skills are learned as they are practised. Sometimes, advice is given, but this is usually done when people work together. The supposedly strong bonds which unite street people seem to be much more a unified front against the straight world than a real fraternal feeling. They understand one another and share the same values and lifestyle. But they also leave one another free to learn the rules of the game on their own, by trial and error, even if error must mean being busted, beaten up, or ripped off.

I made an attempt to find out what type of coaching or help my informants received at the beginning of their career. Bugsy started at thirteen. "It was my birthday," she explained, "and I wanted to get drunk, so I turned a trick." Soon afterwards, she met "this one girl."

> Her and me used to go on double tricks all the time.
> And these two guys that we always went with,

continually ... I mean we went with them about three times a week. This one guy, the guy I was always with, wanted to sit and watch the other two. And Connie, she knew all the positions. And I was watching her and I used to ask her about them.

Photography courtesy of Lincoln Clarkes

(Worldwide Green Eyes)
In Julie's experience, however, the situation is likely to be different:

> You can't work with another girl ... They usually don't want to because it might cut into their business. Young, too ... It's always a new face coming up ... And you don't want to take too much of a chance on her, because you really don't know her.

At the age of fifteen, Jo met somebody "that gave her an idea."

> They just told me that they knew this guy and he was all right. An older business man. He wanted to give me 50 dollars… Then, all of a sudden, it was there, and it was happening, and it was just left to my own discretion.

It is certainly up to each individual to acquire technical competence in whichever manner he or she can contrive to do so. What must be acquired rapidly, however, and over which others have some control, is the knowledge not to endanger the group.

> Some people talk too much. Like, when I first hit the street, I did that all the time. I talked too much, you know, not realizing what I was doing. Until I got told, you know. "Hey, settle down! Keep you mouth shut when the bulls are around!" I never ratted out on anybody but I was talking when there were bulls close by, close enough to listen, and not realizing what I was doing. So, I got it all straightened out, and now when I see a bull, I shut my mouth, no matter what I'm talking about, I just shut right up! (Bugsy)

But patience is reputed to be short on the street, where the pace is fast and people are watchful. Bullshitting, by depicting the world and its occupants, establishing rules of behaviour and describing sanctions for transgression, provides a clear indication of the culture's expectations. It is a didactic tool, flexible and adaptable in content and form, expendable with time and leisure, or rendered as concise and striking as need be.

Gossip, a form of bullshitting focusing on others rather than the self, is seen by Abrahams as a "technique for maintaining community control through the elucidation of public morality." Among the Vincentians where he observed it, he saw it as a means of maintaining in a small community "some kind of community-held public image in the face of internal conflicts and external pressures from the city" (1970:291). Although his informants saw gossip as "potentially disruptive" to both to communal and individual life, they recognized its vital advantage: It gave "a sense of community identity and involvement" (1970:293).

THE DIDACTICS OF STREET TALK

When Bugsy told me of the quarrel she had with her old man, she described the reciprocal duties of an old man and his old lady. To the newcomer to street social organization, she gave several pointers:

> I asked him, I says, "You were out with Pete's old lady?"
> He says, "No." I says "You're a fuckin' liar!" I says, "I was sittin' in the car next to you," I says, "I seen you!" He says, "Well, what were we doing?"
> So I told him! I described it right down to a tee!
> (1)

> He says, "What were you doing at the show?"
> (2)

> I says, "My mark took me to the show. I got paid 400 dollars to go to the show!"
> (3)

He says," Where's the money?" I says, "I spent it!" He says, "On what?" I says, "Junk!" He says, " Oh, you did, did you?" I says, "Yeah!"
(4)

He says, "I gotta go sick, I guess?"
(5)

I says, "Well, go get your other slut there to buy you some!"
(6)

I says, "If she can afford you, if she can afford to go to bed with you,"
(7)

I says, "surely she can afford to buy you one cap of junk!"
(8)

He says, "Here we go!" So I says, "Fuckin' right, here we go!", I says, "Now if you don't mind, I'm busy. Hit it!"
(9)

1.   The offence is double: Her old man has been out (a euphemism for having sexual relations) with a girl who was equally unfaithful since she was somebody's old lady. An old lady owes personal fidelity to her old man, marks, and tricks notwithstanding. The danger and the sanction were also double and, in the second part of the story, there was a free-for-all, with Pete bashing Bugsy's old man and she splitting the lip of Pete's old lady. Moreover, Bugsy and Pete spend the rest of the day together and he bought her dope during that time, probably using his old lady's money to do so. This was fair payment for Bugsy's deeply felt grievance: "He was taking *my* money and spending it on *her!* Buying

her beer and shit. And he was doing it behind my back and every time I asked him about it, he said no, he wasn't!"

2.   Her old man's feeble attempt at suggesting that she may have been as guilty as he was crushed, and Bugsy's virtue and professional integrity were triumphantly established: s

She was working and being well paid for it, too! (Bugsy's usual Homeric proportions, I would suspect). Her answer also reveals to the newcomer that the mark has to pay for the smallest favour: It is his duty, and some women would probably argue that it is his privilege to do so.

3.   Normally, Bugsy would spend the money by scoring for both of them. Yet, nothing has been said about it, and the fact that he had to ask shows that he was not expected to share her dope.

4.   This is the key remark. Bugsy was paying him back for his infidelity by not providing for his needs. He had failed it is duty to her: faithfulness and specific use of her money. So she did not perform hers: bringing him the money she had earned or the dope she had scored. He then had to go sick (do without his fix), which is no small punishment and well befitting the crime.

5.   One could perhaps assume that by being unfaithful, Bugsy's old man has spoilt their relationship and treated *her,* retroactively, as it were, like a slut. I am not sure that there is room for such romantic conceit in Bugsy's anger: It was mostly her pride which was hurt.

6.   This does not mean that the other girl was paying for Bugsy's old man's favours. It may have been meant as an insult since she was comparing him to a pimp. It may also have meant that the "other slut" might as well assume all the responsibilities of an old lady.

7.   To the injury of not bringing dope to her old man, Bugsy added the insult of implying that he was only a one-cap addict. For an old-

timer like Bugsy, this was almost as insulting as accusing him of sniffing glue!

8.　　Bugsy's anger was so well founded that she could even afford to be self- righteous about it.

9.　　The whole scene took place at Bugsy's place of work, in front of a bar, and the last remark was meant to humiliate him even further by stressing the fact that *she,* at least, was doing what she was supposed to do: She was working.

Another important lesson was given by Bugsy at the end of the tale:

> When I was finished with her, *she* didn't look too hot! She had two black eyes and her nose was split all over her face, her mouth was all bleeding, and the cops walked in just as I finished. "What happened here?" And I look at her, as though to say "Oh, hey, say something!", you know. And she says "I was a little bit drunk and I walked into the door as she was opening it." And the cop says "And you didn't know she was behind the door; I guess?" I says "No. I didn't know she was in the bathroom. I don't watch the bathroom," I says, "I'm in here to getting drunk, I ain't here to watching no can, to see who goes in and who comes out!" He says "Yeah", and he says to her "You're sure that's all that's happened?" And she says "Yeah", and then she looked at me! And that was it! And they left.

This is the only time the girl has acted properly. Her last "Yeah" and the look she gave Bugsy were thoroughly enjoyed by the latter, but the listener learns at once that a black eye, a split nose, and a bleeding mouth do not give anyone the right to involve the cops in what is, after all, a well deserved punishment for a transgression to the old man-old lady code of behaviour. The listener also learns that cops are not entirely gullible, but that it does not matter if they do not believe you as long as they do not "have something on" you. In this case, the policeman's suspicions, his disbelief, and his inability to do something about it are evident. Yet, he had to leave because of the lack of corroboration from Pete's old lady. Three pointers are thus given about one's dealings with the police:

(a) "They" can't do anything unless someone rats out or provides proofs; (b) a united front must be presented, whatever the situation; and (c) cops' frustration, while enjoyable, is dangerous; this is not apparent in the story, but the accumulation of such stories eventually leads to the same point made by Dee, Julie, Jo, and Snow in various forms:

- You've beaten them so many times ...
- They don't like that! They don't like to be beat, so they'll show you!
- They hold a grudge ...
- And then, they become "dirty."

In telling me the story, it was probably not Bugsy's intention to describe for me her old man's duty to herself and her duty to him, nor the sanctions which follow a transgression. Yet, she did so—and did so again when she told the story on the street. What actually took place between them is irrelevant to the bullshitting event she performed in the retelling of it. What she *said* took place is all that matters, since it makes sense in terms of the street rules of behaviour. It is a *competent* story.

She has also "laid something on" me at the same time: That she was a good earner and that she was tough. It had already been established in the course of previous interviews that she was on the whole a better earner than I and that she was tougher than I. Now, once again, the exciting street qualities of toughness and smartness (it takes wits to be paid 400 dollars to go to the show) were pitted against the wishy-washy squares whose group I represented. In this case, as often happened in the narratives, a street woman who prided herself on her *smartness* when dealing with square Johns, has shown *toughness* when dealing with her own kind. Milner recognizes those alternatives strategies in the way black men deal with white society: "the devious (trickster) and the open confrontation (bad man)" (Milner 1972b:115). A third person listening to Bugsy telling me the story would have got the double message of street social organization (duties and sanctions) and street-straight opposition.

Having two informants at the same, sitting provided me with a double advantage:

> 1.   They gave each other a knowledgeable audience, thus checking their tendency to bullshit uncontrollably about so-called "facts."
> 2.   They provided each other with an appreciative audience in front of whom to enact the street-straight communication and exchange interaction.

Instead of having two people present at once, I occasionally gave an anonymous transcript to one of the women, asking her to check a detail or give her opinion of the proceedings described in the story. For instance, Julie had once told me that she "packed a 38." When Jo and Snow read and commented on Julie's story of a particular racket she favoured, they could not hide their contempt for someone who had so obviously hinted at a much higher criminal status than her real one, and who had moreover done so in such an unrealistic and unbelievable manner. Julie's claim did not *make sense*.

> - She says she carried a 38, you know ... Someone who carries a 38 is not going to do petty things like that!

> - That's here, isn't it? Now, in the States, I'd have to say yes, but here, no! I've never met anybody in this city, any woman that's carried a gun ... All the different scenes that I've been through in the past years, I've *never* met a woman who walked around packing guns. Was she a hype?
> - *Yes.*
> - Well, now, you couldn't take that risk, because too often you get in a regular run of the mill hassle and getting pulled over and there's no place where you could put a 38: When they stop you,

you know, they might get you to open your coat, your purse, you know. Take your coat and your sweater off and look at your sleeves. Now, where are you gonna have a gun that they're not going to see it? Especially a hype!

After Julie had finished telling me about her racket, I had, rather treacherously, asked a typical "square" question: "Wasn't it dangerous?" And this was when her unfortunate "I always packed a 38!" escaped her. My question called for an outrageous answer, outrageous from the point of view of the logic of competent street behaviour. As Jo and Snow pointed out, a small time female hype, whatever her racket or hustle, does not "pack a 38." Experience shows that it is unpractical and dangerous for her to do so. But my question, stressing my straight attributes: ignorance of street customs, concern for one's safety, fear of danger and excitement, assumption that street activities are all fraught with danger and violence, almost exaggerating them, elicited from Julie the, equally stereotyped reaction of the wild and dangerous gun-packing street hustler. However, Jo and Snow failed to see it as a joke at my expense and simply treated the statement at face value. Since the tall tale was now directed at them and no longer at me, they even took umbrage at the bullshit. Julie's whole story became at once suspicious and they dismissed it entirely, refusing to give her the benefit of the doubt and rejecting the plausibility of her tale and her racket. Reading the story and having to judge it, they saw the statement "I (a Vancouver hype, street hooker, small-time trafficker and hustler) always packed a .38" as an insult to their intelligence and competence as street people. Had Julie been foolish enough to make such a statement to her peers on the street, her sanction would probably have been the same total dismissal she suffered *in absentia* in my office.

Being a constant interviewer and interlocutor, I was very seldom able to observe while receding unobtrusively into the background. I could only accept invitations to lunch or dinner where groups of people would be present, never suggest them. Unless the whole group knew me, as in Protective Custody, a woman would be hesitant to ask me, since she would then impose my presence on the group. Apart from Dee in her group and Brandy in hers, my informants were not leaders. They were either loners or rather meek individuals, in no position, I believe, to impose me on others or to ask me without their stated, or even tacit, consent. I was not important enough to warrant a previous consultation with the group about it, either, since it would then have made the invitation a formal one and the meal a special occasion. Moreover, I believe that the women were not particularly interested in making public knowledge their sessions with me.

This situation naturally reduced my opportunities to see people interact more or less normally. Bugsy and Dee asked me for lunch once, and I accepted the Protective Custody group's invitation to dinner three times and to lunch once. These enabled me to witness the exchange of one-liners and come-backs on several occasions. To me, an uninitiated spectator, they were useful indications of the speaker's status.

To "Up yours!" Dee gave the drawling answer "Sorry, it won't fit!" The challenge, or the establishment of a contest (Goffman 1971:178-179), issued by the first speaker was taken up and successfully met by Dee. It also established the first speaker's status as one tentatively equal to Dee's. The latter's mild come back indicated her acceptance of that status while giving her the last word. It also set the mood of the interchange. In the case of Brandy and Sugar's exchanges, the former's slightly malevolent one-liners confirmed my appreciation of her status. I had already seen an indication of it when Sugar, the cook and person in charge of the meals, always checked with Brandy before issuing her invitations to me. When the fancy took her, Brandy would make such remarks as, "Sugar, cross your legs, it's drafty in here!" These remained scrupulously unanswered, in deference to Brandy's recognized leadership in terms of jail and street experience, as well as in terms of sheer personality. Moreover, Brandy scornfully explained later, "It's *true!* She smells and she knows it."

The measure of the street is constantly taken. Life there is dangerous and, lest it should be forgotten and people become complacent and careless, reminders are given in the form of stories such as the one Bugsy spontaneously told me one day. As well as a stern warning that it is unwise to have dealings with the big guys and to rip off one's business associates, it is a nice piece of folklore meting out horror and humour in an almost unbeatable combination.

- Did you know about Harry B. being killed? Who was strangled with a pair of women's panty hose? Last year? And Hurst? That's another guy.
- *Porky?[12]*
  - Yeah, Porky! Well, there was those three, Harry, and Porky, and Rocky ... They all got it, the same three. Harry was the one who was strangled in his mother's backyard. And Rocky, they found his body, and it took them two weeks to identify him. Whoever did him in did a good job. They pulled out all his teeth, put arson on his fingers and on his toes ...
- *Put arson?*

-Burnt his fingers, you know ... and ... oh, they just destroyed him completely, so that there was no way to identify him. His mother identified him by his heart ... He had a heart-shaped mole on his ass ... Heart-shaped! Lots of people got moles, but they didn't figure anybody would come with that! And Rocky's mom and dad had gone out of town. And they came back unexpectedly. And when they couldn't find Rocky, they went down to the Morgue. They couldn't identify him by his face because he had acid poured all over his face, so they turned him over and she said: "Yeah'"

---

[12]   Since my status was ambiguous, a total outsider, yet under the apparent auspices of the Authorities, no amount of knowledge or ignorance I might show surprised them. So Bugsy found it natural that I should know at once the nickname of a junkie killed the year before (yet the ethnocentric assumption that such knowledge is probably shared by everyone would not play in the case of a total square).

All three of them were drug addicts. The guys that did that are guys from the States. There's two guys from Canada serving time for it and they didn't do it. Four guys from the States ... in the Mafia. Some guys in the Mafia from the States. They gave Harry B. and Rocky the money to go and pick them up an ounce. And they say: "If you don't come back, you're not going to live to see tomorrow!" Well, they came back and said: "We got ripped off!" They had the money stashed. So these guys say: "Well, you've got one week to come up with the money." And when the week was up, that was it! The guys came down; they were hiding; they found them.' They were watchin' them.

The presence of the "guys in the Mafia from the States" puts the blame on *outsiders,* thus strengthening the bonds among *insiders.* This is particularly important in this case since the alternative interpretation would be that insiders (the "two guys from Canada" now "serving time for it") were in fact guilty of the deed. By the same token, the injustice of Justice is also alluded to, always a useful lesson.

In spite of the real dangers evoked in the last story, it is understood that you should not allow the fear of potential dangers to interfere with the conduct of your business on the street. You should always be ready to take chances. Such a story was told by Bugsy who, for once and to her mortification, was unwilling to overlook the "funny feeling" she had about a customer.

Well, I know one girl ... I turned down a trick, and he asked her, and she went out with him. And she got 200 dollars for it! It was true, very true, I know she wouldn't lie to me. If she would have lied to me, I woulda hit her! I hate somebody who lies, I do! And she says: "You know, that trick that you turned down?" She says: "I got 200 dollars from him'" I says: "You didn't!" She says: "I did. Really!" She showed it to me ... and she hadn't worked all night, and she had no money on her when she came downtown. "You bitch! I want half! I turned him down for you!" She had the choice of giving it to me or I'd take it! My best friend goes out and turns him! I told her, I says: "Ah, I don't like him!" She says: "Well, if I'm not down in 16 minutes, come up and get me." She was down in 10 minutes. She got 200 dollars for it! I asked her: "Did you rob him?" She says "No". I says: "Are you sure?" "No". The guy walked by, patted her on the ass and he said: "I had a good time," he says, "see you, baby!" O.K. ... Oh, wow! That pissed me off!

One should not take too seriously Bugsy's threats to her friend. The woman was after all her "best friend." However, she was not entirely kidding either. The story ends as foreseen, Bugsy remaining the heroine: She gets her half and all ends well, with two *caps* each and a meal in a restaurant.

Beyond the preliminary search for identification and assertion of *bona fides,* provided by the establishment of who you are, whom you know and who knows you, what you know about them, and the acknowledgement of insider's status, bullshitting maps out very clearly, in my somewhat limited sampling of tales, the following rules of behaviour.

1. *Rights and duties* of street people, such as those described in Bugsy's story where the old lady was defined as a provider, and where solidarity against the police, whatever intestine dissention there may have been, was stressed;

2. *Sanctions for transgression,* as in the story describing the fate of Harry and Rocky, who had attempted to rip off their business partners, or the one about Bugsy's punitive measures against her unfaithful old man;

3. *Ranking* among street people, sometimes established, as in Dee and Brandy's case, by the use of one-liners;

4.   *Dealings with the police:* Other stories treat such topics as how to beware of Morality Squad cops, of newcomers on the street, of rip offs; how to deal with a trick's wife; what to expect of marks and how far to go with them; how aloof one must always be with "good cops"; how to handle drunks, perverts, East Indians—described further as *villains;* how to foil the narcs.

This is a vitally important conduct, which is formalized in narrative description. These stories are told for their entertainment value and to help pass the time of day. Their role is also to establish the teller as someone with experience and knowledge, tighten the bonds of the community, strengthen stereotypes, and create folk heroes and villains. They can be amusing, fearsome, or sad. They are stories through which new comers are instructed and group members keep their values alive.

Mutual story telling and the various forms of bullshitting form a transaction known as *conversation,* in the course of which reality is constantly redefined.

The most important vehicle of reality-maintenance is conversation. One may view the individual's everyday life in terms of the working away of a conversational apparatus that ongoingly *[sic]* maintains, modifies and reconstructs his subjective reality ... It is important to stress, however, that the greater part of reality-maintenance in conversation is implicit, not explicit. Most conversation does not in so many words define the nature of the world. -Rather, it takes place against the background of a world that is silently taken for granted. (Berger and Luckmann, 1967:152).

CHAPTER FIVE

STREET AND STRAIGHT:

CONTRASTING CHARACTERISTICS

The characters perceived by my informants and depicted in their stories are clearly divided into two main groups: Street and Straight. Through characterization and stereotyping, rigid boundaries are created between them. Verbal manipulations performed by street people on straights or squares base their technique on cultural interpretations of the squares' characteristics. Without the street woman's certainty that a mark is, by definition, greedy and stupid, she could not have elaborated her method for handling him. In this sense, definitions serve as interactional guidelines. There are visible boundaries between the two groups: They speak and dress differently, their means of livelihood are different, their lifestyle is different. In addition to this objectively evident contrast, my informants also perceive a corresponding ideal separation: values and life experience.

SQUARES, ROUNDERS, AND THE JAIL EXPERIENCE

The paragon of straight life is the square or square John. According to Rumack (1972), "a square is a person who does not possess a police record." More than a simplistic definition, it is, by street standards, an erroneous one: there are squares in jail, and there are square crimes as well. Were I to commit a fraud and be convicted of it, I would not *ipso facto* change sides. Squareness is much more than a legal definition, but jail experience is certainly an important factor in determining the characteristics of both groups. As well as crimes typically committed by squares, there are also square criminals, who do not live on the street, who are married, have children, and lead a conventional life. Their way of thinking, explains Dee, "is different from ours. Their life is the same as yours, yet they know a way of ours. Like, it's mixed between the two." Since possessing (or not) a police record is only an official recognition and sanction of a certain type of behaviour, it is not surprising that it should not play an exclusive part in the definition of a square. It must also be understood that a square's lack of involvement in illegal activities is not necessarily due to his honesty: Many street people may see him as simply careful or pusillanimous. The lawfulness of his conduct is certainly one of the factors which serve to define him, but Rumack's privative definition is not only insufficient, it is also partially unfounded. Letkeman's definition is much more comprehensive since it regards lifestyle as a most important component:

> Criminals use the term "square" to refer to (1) the conventional citizen committed to the legitimate lifestyle, and who is stable and reliable, and (2) the one-time offender otherwise committed to a legitimate lifestyle (Letkeman 1971:110).

To the *square* John, the Street usually opposes the *rounder.* This linguistic opposition between the terms serves to illustrate a cultural opposition almost as visually as black and white do for other groups.

The person "out of line" is normally defined as a *deviant;* however, the power of naming and defining has been granted to those who, in this case, are themselves straight.

> Honest folk give names to things, and the things bear these names ... I am aware that honest people are also objects to each other. I am given names ... But if I am named, I name in turn. Thus, naming and being named, I lived in a state of reciprocity. Words are thrown at me, I catch them and throw them at others (Sartre 1963:40-41).

The straight naming process makes the object what it has been named—in this case a *deviant*, a *criminal*. By this naming, "their failings and errors are transformed into a permanent predisposition, that is into a destiny" (Sartre 1963:34). There is no true naming reciprocity between straight and street people. Street naming is almost powerless to affect and metamorphose straight people into their definition. Literally and metaphorically, straight people are seldom reached by the language of the street. Yet, they must acknowledge the name given to them by street people as the derogatory term and the branding mechanism it is. And they must also accept the name given to themselves by street people as a self-praising definition. In this article on folk ideas and worldview, Dundes (1971) discusses the opposition of line and circle: the *positive* connotation of *linearity,* evident in the expressions "straight" talk, getting "straightened" out or "squared" away after having got "out of line" is opposed to the *negative* connotation of the *circle,* also evident in the expressions "circular" reasoning, "roundabout" ways of speaking, "going around in circles." But he points out a recent reversal of these connotations.

> Recently, the line versus the circle opposition has taken a new turn. It has been restated in terms of straight versus groovy. Curves mean "curvaceous" and sex; lines mean "straight" or "square" and the denial of sex. There is a movement away from the "straight and narrow" towards the "groovy and broad" (Dundes 1971:99).

Thus it is not surprising that street people have defined outsiders as *straight* people and *square* Johns, and insiders' as *rounders.* A rounder is "someone who has business on the street," said Dee who described those in the "fast life" as people who

> Hang around the Corner, are into different things, are always on the go ... They are generally rounders.

Julie has them

Hang around in bars, and you see them on the street as well. And they probably know a lot about what's happening, you know, if you go up and talk to them.

A relatively newcomer to the street, Tiny listed the straight people seen on the street:

Tricks, marks, common shoppers. They're not even there! And rounders. They know everything. But they're not involved.

Yet, if their degree of participation and commitment is not unanimously agreed upon, they are uniformly thought to be knowledgeable about the ways of the street, and usually trustworthy. For Snow and Jo, rounders are the successful ones on the street:

You know, there are people out there collecting pop bottles. And there's the ones that are making hundreds and thousands of dollars a day. Those are the rounders.

When I asked them if *they* were rounders, they answered yes only after the briefest hesitation

Rumack (1972) defines the rounder as "A person who has spent time in jail or who is engaged in an illegal activity. All the girls whom I met considered themselves Rounders." Only Brandy, among my informants, would agree with his narrow definition. For her, rounders are simply "criminals" and the "top men" are those who don't get caught. Participation in illegal activities and jail terms, once again, is not seen by the informants as figuring predominantly in the definition of rounders, except perhaps for Brandy who has spent half her life in jail. However, the fact that all Rumack's informants claim rounder status is quite significant. Here again, Letkeman's definition seems much more pertinent:

The most common distinction made by the offender is between the "rounder" and the "square" (or "square-john"). "Rounder", however, has different connotation than "criminal." Simply to be labelled a criminal by the court does not confer rounder status. To be a rounder one must be known and recognized as one, by other rounders and by persons seriously committed to the illegitimate lifestyle. In fact, inmates of prisons refer to some other inmates as "squares." (1971:110)

Bugsy's definition of a rounder explains the prestige conferred by the title:

Someone who's been around a long time, knows the street up and down, knows who are the cops. They are solid people: They don't rat out to the cops. They don't have to!

Rumack and Letkeman's definitions are important here since they are Canadian definitions, an exception in a predominantly American field of study, and since they reflect the terminology used in two large Canadian cities. The informants themselves stress the fact that American and Canadian terms vary.

If Rumack's definition were adequate, he would hardly feel it necessary to mention that all his informants "considered themselves Rounders," since, as prostitutes just out of jail, they would automatically qualify for the title. What the statement indicates is the prestige attached to the term and the eagerness of informants to be identified with the "solid people."

In the past, when *dope fiends* were despised exceptions and criminals were professionals, the distinction was clearly made. According to Old Sal, Jackson's old-timer addict:

Police gave us that name, characters. In them days we was people. Folks was squares and we was people. The police had a lot of respect for the characters, they only rode the people that shot dope. Characters tended to their own business (Jackson 1972:72).

Going to jail is a part of street life and, as such, may count little as a formal marker (not like being a hype, for instance). It only bestows the title of *con* or *ex-con,* with its connotation of particular experience and membership in an additional subculture. But, for most street people, one is either in jail, has been in jail, or will probably soon be in jail, and the continuity of life is not broken through the passage in jail, however unpleasant the experience may be. It does not change people, their lifestyle, their values as radically as, for instance, being a hype does. Brandy, an old time con, says: "I got a good home in the street, but jail is part of life; it doesn't faze me."

Not only can jail be for some a necessary physical respite (with medical and nutritional advantages), is also strengthens bonds by adding an extra dimension to group inclusion. Julie mentioned several times the warm, if superficial, feeling experienced when someone known "in here" is later met on the street, a result presumably of the "relaxed socialization" which Preble and Casey (1969:8) see as being centred around the "facts and folklore" of the heroin user's life on the street.

Since a stay in jail figures extensively in straight definitions, one must remember that concern with the legality of one's actions is indeed a typically straight notion. The street people's initial encounter with the criminal justice system is often reduced to being "hassled" or being "busted," and this may well be how they define the border between activities that are marginally lawful (and only cause you to be hassled) and those that are illegal (and enable *them* to bust you).

The common belief that "there's a law for the rich [and also the straight] and a law for the poor [and also street people]" perhaps leads to the ineptitude or indifference of some women in protecting themselves. It is true that, like Stoddart's informants, whose knowledge of the requirements of the law enabled them to manipulate the format of their transactions, the women I interviewed are informed of the legal technicalities surrounding the possession of narcotics and trafficking in drugs. As prostitutes, however, all but one misunderstood their legal status. Bugsy, for instance, after eight years as a prostitute, did not really know what part of her transactions caused her delinquency. She did not alter her *modus operandi* in 1972 when the charges against prostitutes changed from "vagrancy" to "soliciting." She believed that soliciting, which is in fact the offence, means "selling your body for sex," not an illegal endeavour in Canada. As far as she was concerned, she "propositioned" her clients, minded her own business, and hoped to be left alone. The many tactics used by women (Layton 1975:201-202; 1979) to protect themselves from the law or even to try and operate within the wording of article 195.1 of the *Criminal Code* on soliciting for the purpose of prostitution, have been so unsuccessful that a definite bitterness is felt against the police, who are moreover accused of "turning everything around" in their testimony.

CONTRASTING LIFESTYLES

Street and straight people are differentiated and contrasted by the life they lead far more than by their involvement in criminal activities or their legitimate occupations. Squares are seen as engaged in the dreary routines of "nine-to-five" jobs. Their social life and their pleasures are perceived as equally dull:

> Straight people, you know, they go out once a week, twice a week for dinner, to the bars for a few drinks, and they sit at home and watch T.V. We're downtown all the time, you know, and there's nothing big about going for a drink or anything! (Sue)

As well as stressing the lackluster square way of life, the inability of street people to cope with the demands of a straight occupation was also mentioned. Moreover, if they are heroin addicts, as so many of them are, they cannot support their habit on a straight salary. "They couldn't afford to be a junkie on a job. They might hold a job, but they'd need to boost, or something" (Dee).

The pace of street life, as well, would not allow a junkie to hold the conventional "nine-to-five."

You can't stay stabilized as a straight job and be, you know, running downtown and scoring, plus the fact that the money isn't enough ... You'd have to have a high paying job, and you couldn't hold it, not running around looking for the people that you need. (Julie)

Instead, she explains,

If you're hooking and you're using, you go out and make money half way through the night, score for the morning, continue working. So that when you wake up in the daytime, you'd have stuff to fix.

One only has to listen to Bugsy describe how she spends her day to understand the total incompatibility of the two lifestyles:

I do my first trick, then I score. I fix, then I do another trick, and then I score two caps and fix. Every trick I do, I score. I spend all my money unless I'm loaded enough that I want to hold on, so that I can buy a couple of caps to take home. Usually at the end of the night, I have about $120 and I score enough to take home. I usually quit around six in the morning.

The men she meets in the early morning are all straight. Yet, she clearly shows the difference between their "straight" reasons for being on the street at that time, and hers.

They are people who drive all the time: Guys who work late at night, or guys who come into town, loggers or something, or guys who have been out for something to eat, or have been at a party or something. There are four or five of us at that time of night.

The fear of the street often felt by straight people was mentioned to me. Julie's straight parents were terrified by it and thought they would get "mugged or raped, or something," if they went "there." Yet, she stresses how "normal" street life is, with people "eating and sleeping, like everywhere else!" Dee also cannot stress enough that "we think of our life as normal. To us, it's normal, it's our formal way of life." Talking of her friends and acquaintances, she says, "They live on the street because they do business there, their friends are on the street, and that's their big living room. (Dee)

To the straight life described by Sue, Dee opposes that of the hypes:

> They like the excitement that's on the Corner, they like night life, they like the excitement ... They like the excitement of being either a dealer or a junkie, of playing cat and mouse with the bulls. You've got to like all this to become a hype. To be a real junkie, you've got to like it, because if you don't, you'll never make it down there.

As one of Coutts' matrons admits: "A real live game of cops and robbers, an exciting life, and how tame everything else must be in comparison!" (Coutts 1961:101).

Agar (1973:1) refers to previous studies of addiction which mostly "assume the social psychological failure status of the addict as the problem to be explained" and challenges this assumption. Preble and Casey go further still. For them, heroin does not provide for its lower class users "a euphoric escape from the psychological and social problems which derive from ghetto life." It provides, on the contrary,

> A motivation and rationale for the pursuit of a meaningful life, albeit a socially deviant one. The activities these individuals engage in and the relationships they have in the course of their quest for heroin are far more important than the minimal analgesic and euphoric effects of the small amount of heroin available to them (Preble and Casey 1969:

VALUES AND ATTITUDES

Some characteristics of the two groups were better defined than others by my informants, What was less well known (the straight world) tended to fall into stereotypes and lack the grey shades of what was more familiar to them (the street world) about which statements were usually qualified. Street and straight people were contrasted in almost every one of their activities. Their values and attitudes were constantly opposed and no doubt was left that street ways were superior. The essential differences between the two constantly contrasted protagonists were described as touching on the basic quality of their lives: freedom *vs* constraint, competence *vs* ignorance, generosity *vs* greed.

In opposition to the sedentary and secure square Johns, the unlawfulness of the street people's occupations dictates many constraints in their life, such as the requirement of mobility and the need for privacy.

> Most people don't like too many people knowing where they're staying ... People that you're close to or you're friends with, they usually know where you live ... Like, just everybody on the street wouldn't know where I was living, and yet there're might be ten people that know where I am. Like,all the people that buy off me, there's a few that know where I live, but mostly, I show up when I show up!

> You move often, just to keep ahead of the police and too many people get to know where I live and they're coming all hours of the night (that's if you're a dealer). Lots of people live in rooms on a monthly basis, or weekly. (Dee)

This freedom of movement is accompanied by an independence from many conventional constraints which was sometimes expressed in direct contrast to the square Johns' concern with his neighbours' opinion and his fear of stepping over the conventional boundaries of straight propriety.

> Like you, for instance, if you thought: "Oh, geez, I think I'd like to tattoo!" You'd think: "Well, maybe the woman next door would think I'm .. " Where the con doesn't think that, you know. "Hell with the person or what he thinks! If he doesn't like it, that's *my* arm!" (Dee)

Dee was the first to admit that everyone on the Corner was not necessarily "smart," but she saw them all competent enough in the ways of the street to survive and enjoy their lifestyle, even if they were not like the "good junkie" who is "self sufficient." In opposition to this knowledge, we find the square John's ignorance.

> A square John walking down the street couldn't pick four hypes out of a dozen. If there's a dozen people there and four of them are hype, you wouldn't be able to pick them out. Another hype would pick them out! (Dee)

She also described a woman shopper walking down the street: "She walks with her attention on herself, she is not interested in people around her ... a hype would be! She only looks at shop windows."
Snow, in contrast, described a hype, forever anxious not to miss anything, and indicated to the uninitiated how being attentive and observant usually pays off:

> If you don't look, you're gonna miss something. Like, I notice someone lurking in a doorway and I think: "What's that guy? Is he looking for a girl or is he ..." I was watching. "He's up to something! So, I'll just watch him for a while." And, sure enough! You know, like, say prior to that I had money and I was gonna, say, buy some dope, right? But I just held back. I wanted to watch this person. Sure enough, some

trafficker comes by and that guy jumps on top of him
with another partner! Of nowhere, right?"

When this plain ignorance of street mores and the inability to read clues express themselves, they take on another quality: "Ignorant means obnoxious. Straight people are ignorant to your kind of life, to the street scene. They don't know anything about it." (Sugar) "Ignorant means obnoxious" is the street version of the straight statement that "ignorance of the law is no excuse." Lack of knowledge and understanding leads to an "obnoxious" behaviour. This behaviour itself is seen as "ignorant." "Ignorant cops: They have no manners at all! They say 'There's a prostitute,' or 'There's a slut,' or something stupid like that." (Bugsy) Equally ignorant are some policemen to whom *freaks* are reported. "Most of them just laugh at you and say 'Well, it's your own fault for being a prostitute!'" (Bugsy)

Straight people's ignorance and obnoxious behaviour are well established. Their main characteristic, however, is not that, but greed. Greed is indeed what causes them to become marks. A mark is defined by Maurer (1940:119) as someone who must have "larceny in his veins, who wants something for nothing." If such a man has money, he is a con man's ideal prey. Klockars' expert, Swaggi, draws from his experience to confirm this assessment:

Any hustler can tell you that 9 out of 10 people got larceny. Maybe even 99 out of 100 ... If the price is right and a man can use the merchandise, he's gonna buy. No question about it (Klockars 1974:62).

In my experience, women have just as much larceny in them as men. May be more (Klockars 1974:49).

My informants are unanimous and adamant about the truth of statements such as these. Dee, talking about boosting, said she never had any problem selling the stolen merchandise at about one third of its retail price. She claimed to have solicited people in bars and beer parlours.

"Usually people will buy from [boosters]. Especially square Johns. They're glad to get a good deal!"

The women's experience with square Johns explains their feelings, since they usually enter with them into a mutually exploitative relationship. The following dialogue (my questions in italics) was one of several where the terms of straight-street transactions were defined.

- *What do they want from you?*
- *[Bitterly]* All of us!... It depends, sometimes they want company
- Sometimes, they just want to be with you and find out how you live, how the other half lives, how you're doing.
- *Like me!*
- You know, they do! They say, "We're observing you."
- Some just want a party.
- Some want... Like I said, company. Company into clubs, bars, you know?
- *If the price is right, are you willing to give them what they want? Or will you always to give a little less for the same money?*
-I always try to get a little bit more!
- *More money, rather than give less?*
- Right!
- Well, I don't like to give any, really, but I know they're got money, and I know I can get money, I stick with them, you know. (Jo and Snow)

They want something, or they just want to screw me and they don't want to give me money. They're trying to do something... (Jo)

As Jo and Snow indicate, curiosity as well as greed properly speaking may be the basis for a mark or a trick's desire to purchase the services or company of street women. This is particularly true for heroin addicts:

He wanted to watch me ... He wanted to see, you know, to see the whole nitty-gritty right there, that he'd heard about and he's seen on T.V. And then, when I got it, his eyes were just *bulging!* (Julie)

Julie, who often met older men "out for a good time," told stories about them and depicted them rubbing their hands, leering, and thinking: "Well, Jesus Christ! There, the old lady's at home, and I get me a young whippersnapper here!"

To the square John's exploitative greed, curiosity, or lust is opposed the rounder's generosity. In the context of the junkie's world, this usually means giving someone money to score or dope to fix. This is normally done for friends, not for acquaintances or associates.

If she's good ... I mean not just anybody, but people I consider friends, that I know would do the sane for me if I was in the same, you know ...(Jo)

If she had money and knew I didn't have any, and I was getting sick, she'd split .. That'd be out of friendship. I've done it 101 times for her! I'm a sucker for fixin' people! (Bugsy)

This occasional willingness to share mentioned by my informants does not however seem to be the rule everywhere among heroin users. Another feeling is sometimes expressed, even among partners: "I'm looking out for myself. I might be sick tomorrow; anyway, he's got something working for him that I don't know about." (Preble and Casey 1968:8)

My informants did not explain this apparent discrepancy. I would assume that the more limited means of livelihood open to women (prostitution being the one to which they most often resort) and their usually more restricted involvement in criminal activities may account to some extent for their apparent greater generosity: If their friends had "something working for" them, they would probably know about it. Hence, the need expressed is genuine. Moreover, the necessity for prostitutes to be visible on the street makes it easy for the lender to claim her due when her turn comes to be in need. For it is always implied that the reciprocity of the gift is expected.

There appears to be a curious mixture of disregard for short range needs, such as tomorrow's fix now available and given away, and a long range concern for undated future needs, such as some other day's fix lacking and expected back. Since junkies usually live very much for the present, this apparent contradiction may be an indication of their solidarity. It is however no more than an apparent contradiction, since this loan is made while their own needs are being satisfied, the present is taken care of, and the future seems far away.

ADDICTS, NON-ADDICTS, AND TIME ORIENTATION

Not all street people are drug addicts, although many of them do take drugs. Yet, users form the core of street life. A strong solidarity exists among them and they have acquired a prestige denied to them in the past, when good citizens and criminals both frowned upon drug addiction. Jackson (1972:72) quotes Big Sal: "You didn't shoot dope back in them days. If you shot dope you was a sorry, rotten, no-good bitch, it was strictly uh-uh, you didn't shoot or sniff dope or anything. If you did, you wasn't no good."

Fifteen years before my research there, Oakalla had a small section reserved for drug addicts who were separated from the rest of the inmates. They now form a very large proportion of the jail population. Jo's first estimate from "nearly all" became upon reflection "70-80 per cent." They also form a recognized group and act as one. One staff member commented: "The hypes always put pressure on everybody ... The hypes are bloody big heroes around here:" With the increased number and the increased prestige and acceptance of its members by other street people, the heroin addict subculture and its values tend to affect even non-using street familiars.

The need to live exclusively in the present is part of the junkies' life. Their needs are pressing and immediate. The "straightening out" provided by the drug relieves anxiety and restores peace and optimism. The hard-core junkie lives almost exclusively to fix. I once asked Bugsy, barely out of her teens, whether she had any fun.

> On the street? That's hard to say ... If I wasn't using, I believe I could have a lot of fun. But when I'm using, I don't have any fun. My mind's too set on getting money to fix. That's it!

As Jo and Snow described their hit-and-run technique, it became evident that they were only concerned with immediate profits and were not ready to plan more profitable hustles if those required some delay. They joked: "Well, our needs are bigger now! Anyway, there's always money around." This is a belief shared by all my informants. Marks are there for the picking. They will be there again tomorrow, and again they will provide. All windfalls are seen in the same light:

> Everybody, pretty well, is on Welfare. Oh, the day you get your Welfare cheque, you go down and score 3-4 caps, and then your Welfare cheque's gone and you don't worry again for another month! It's easy money for a day ... It's a hooker's day off! (Dee)

The future is not something junkies feel particularly anxious to delve into. They face rip-offs, beatings, a diminishing ability to provide for their needs, and overdoses which are sometimes fatal. Based on their experience of everyday life on the street, they could only too well anticipate a possible future of their own, and it appears that they would rather overlook what they can foresee. Moreover, the drug fixes their mind on the urgency of their needs and their immediate satisfaction. Using prostitutes tend to shrug off mentions of the future. The non-addicted prostitutes, on the other hand, are reputed by my informants to have a different attitude, and this difference appears to be enough for the street group to attribute to them straight values, in spite of a lifestyle that a straight observer would have some difficulty accepting as his own. It is thought that their ambition is to get off the street and, possibly, become call girls. Since call girls are thought to have legitimate occupations as well, it is not surprising that most of my informants saw non-using prostitutes in their role as aspiring call girls as almost square, if not in their lifestyle and knowledge of the street, at least in their desire for security and improved working conditions.

Dee believed that their ambition to become call girls is accompanied by a liking of the lifestyle that presumably, (since neither she nor her friends actually know any call girls), goes with it. "They like that. They enjoy being wined and dined, where the ordinary street girl doesn't enjoy that." Julie's description of non-using prostitutes presumed a desire to build up a clientele. For instance, they are usually believed to avoid ripping off their customers. If they need extra money, they are more likely to turn an extra trick. They also little to do with fences. In other words, they conduct their business as legitimately as possible, with an eye to improving their lot.

They are said to observe some of the street rules of behaviour even if not belonging on the street, such as keeping an eye out for problems. Because their outlook is seen as basically different, they may however be viewed with some suspicion.

> Yeah, they're good, they're good about warning. They're helping ... But only as far as the heat's concerned, and if they had a bad trick ... They don't like junkies, most of them ... The users are very leery of them. I mean, they're on their guard. You know, they're not users, and you don't know whether they're sincerely hooking ... and they could be watching everything, right? (Julie)

Because of their lesser involvement in criminal activities and their different life orientation, both due to their outsider status in the "drug scene," non-addict prostitutes are partly assimilated to straight people.

The basic oppositions between *now* and *later,* the *present* and the *future,* help to distinguish between the immediate concerns of the street and the planning of the straight world. But equally important to understand is the concept of a dichotomy of the present as it may be perceived by the addicts. There seems to exist two opposite aspects of the present, as it is lived on the street by addicts. A *normalized present* is clearly perceived, one where needs are momentarily satisfied and things are again in order. Language indicates that being under the influence of heroin is normal. For instance, one is "sick" when one needs the drug and one "fixes" in order to "straighten out." To this present reinstated by the drug into normality, the street opposes the concept of another, almost *anomic present,* where every thought converges on the regaining of this normality.

In the first case, all needs are satisfied for the present and the immediate future. The addict may then revert to what Dundes describes, in opposition to the peasant cultures analyzed by Foster (1967), as the larger, North American culture's belief in a principle of unlimited good, a culture where prevails the belief that "there's plenty more where that came from." (Dundes 1971:96) In the second case, the pressure to satisfy their needs is such that the addict can only believe the glaring evidence of *that* money, *that* dope, *that* trick, as being the ones which must at once be stolen or turned, since no other will serve to fulfill present yearnings as fast as those would. "You would understand that I'm sick and that I need that money," explained Jo's friend, and I believe that indeed what is meant is not just that she needs money, but that she needs *that* money, where *that* simply means *now*.

STREET AND STRAIGHT VILLAINS

There are definitely other villains around, but Street folklore provides four easily identifiable villains: (1) the street villain, the *rip off;* (2) the marginal villain, the *rat,* sometime classified as an acey-ducey; (3) the straight villain, the *East Indian;* although villainous characteristics are also found among all "bad tricks," the East Indian is the one who embodies them all in a fashion best suited to fulfill the street's sense of horror and drama; and (4) the ultra-straight *narc,* or arch-villain.

The Rip Off

Rip offs are street people. It is also usually street people who are *ripped off*. The same action performed on a square John is more likely to be called a robbery and no particular stigma is attached to it. Indeed, on the contrary, if the robbery is performed with wit and elegance, or at least with impetuosity and recklessness, it becomes a topic for boasting. Although a trick can also be ripped off, the word is mostly used for street people: "When you talk about a square John, you say you 'robbed' him" (Sue). A few seconds later, she added with a hesitant laugh: "You rip off your friends!" Her reservations may have been due to the fact that rip offs, although remaining street people, cease to be friends.

Jo describes what she refers to as her "code of moral ethics" (her intonation puts the words between quotation marks):

> Like, I won't think nothing of taking from a trick or something in that type of situation. Or boosting in stores , or in a general con thing. But I wouldn't take from my own kind. And I wouldn't rob my friends, although my friends should understand ... You know, people tell me: "If you're my friend, you should understand that I'm sick and that I need that money." Well, you should ask me, and maybe I'll give it to you!

> I wouldn't do that because I could never go back to them. I'd be too ashamed ... There's times I've got awfully desperate and I've been awfully crazy ... Still, I haven't gone and robbed by friends ... And I've done a lot of things!

If Bugsy's story of Harry and Rocky (Chapter Four) is unusually sympathetic towards them, it is probably because they ripped off the "guys from the Mafia, from the States," twice outsiders. My informants' experience is usually with small time rip offs;

Sometimes they wait for you outside when they see you have a trick, and they threaten you ... even with a knife, so you have to give them your money. (Bugsy)

They are often junkies who stand in the Corner and try to intimidate you. (Dee)

They can either out and rob you, or sell you blank caps, or just take your money and disappear. Usually it's from a dope dealer you get a rip off. (Sue)

Peter Reilly in a *Fifth Estate* television special (CTV, March 15, 1977), reporting on the seventy-five drug-related murders, acknowledged as such by the police, which have taken place in Vancouver over the previous twenty years, mentions the satisfaction expressed by street junkies after the execution of well known rip offs.

There are stories prevalent in the oral tradition which relate the deeds of rip offs. When the narrator is also the victim, threats are issued, reminiscent of grade B gangster movies or old melodramas: "He won't live to see tomorrow" or, by Bugsy: "This guy ripped me off and I'll see him in his grave." However, as bitterly resented as rip offs are, their actions are seemingly understood. I was told once: "Dog eat dog," and many times: "It's a jungle, out there!"

The Rat

Not only are rats as hated as rip offs, they are also despised. One of the questions I had asked Sugar led her to talk about her being held in Protective Custody. She said: "I'm in here because I'm supposed to be a *rat* ...," mimicking all the loathing on her face and in her voice that such an accusation would generate when made by other street people.

Yet, without rats, many people who are arrested would have to face their own responsibility for their arrest. Instead, they can rest secure in the belief (or, at least, the expression of the belief) that, had they not been ratted on, they would still be free. Their own skills remain essentially unchallenged since they cannot be held responsible for the unfair advantage taken over them.

> It's worse to be a rat than a rip off. Most of us wouldn't be in here if it wasn't for them. (Sue)

> The next thing I knew, there was six narc bulls and four policemen down there! I know who did it. And when she does come in, she better move into (my) group, because then they can take her out again and bury her. I don't care! But she won't live very long. She put too many people in here ... (Bugsy)

I once mentioned to Bugsy that I had not seen for quite some time a woman I knew in front of a small Granville street hotel where she worked, and was wondering if she was all right. She answered scornfully:

> Maybe somebody put cement boots on her. She's wrong. She's a rat. Maybe they put swimming boots on her. If they did, she deserved it. She's been working for the cops. She's never been busted.

Julie, describing the technique employed by the police to invite people to rat out on their associates, concluded:

> It helps in some cases [to rat], maybe, for yourself. But, believe me, it's not a quiet world. And if you're sure you're gonna rat, you might as well be sure you're not gonna use junk anymore, and that's because ... You know, it always comes out in the wash!

Unlike rip offs, rats are excluded from the community: The classification reveals that they are unanimously put by the informants with the Police group. As mentioned in the second chapter, I gave the informants some 200 cards bearing a word taken out of the texts and intuitively felt to be relevant to the culture and asked them to put these cards into groups that "made sense" to them (see Appendices A and B). The four or five initial groups were then subdivided and further refined. The only surprise I had was to see "rat" put unhesitatingly in the first round with "cop," "bull," "pig," "narc," "probation officer," "matron," "jail," "judge," and other people representing the "Authority" group. Narrowing down definitions on the second and third regrouping, it remained with "narc," "pig," and "bull." Neither rip offs nor rats are in an enviable position: as street-defined deviants among straight-defined deviants, they are rejected by both cultures.

The East Indian[i]

The negative characteristics of certain visible groups are sweepingly established and members of these groups are normally branded as villains. The villain stereotype also makes it impossible for these people to be treated otherwise. The folk characterization of the East Indian trick, for instance, prevents the "nice" East Indian, who is said to exist, if only as an exception, from being treated in a friendly manner.

> You don't want to be seen having a beer with them because they might call you "Hindu lover." (Bugsy)

> He *[her East Indian mark]* came here *[Oakalla]* ... Well, shit: I almost got laughed out of the whole building, hey! (Julie)

The reputation of East Indians is unmatched by any other group of customers: "East Indians are the ones you're supposed to stay most away from" (Sue).

> Oh, boy, they do some terrible things! I hate them guys with a passion! They're terrible! They've done things like taking a light bulb and stuck it up a girl, and hit her in the stomach and shatter the light bulb; or take a broken bottle and shove it up her. They've killed a few girls, slashed them up, left them bleeding ... Or they

get a girl up to a room ... if she's a new girl, she doesn't know and she'll go up to a room, and he'll have six or seven of his friends there, and they'll just keep her in the room all night. They usually take all the money she's already got. (Sue)

Sue is not a prostitute, and she has often declined to answer questions pertaining to prostitutes and prostitution, pleading her lack of first hand knowledge—the same lack of personal experience she would have in the case of East Indian tricks. Yet, she was willing to talk, about them at length. As to Bugsy, her indignation was such that she for once forgot her usual modesty in my presence:

East Indians cheat a lot ... They try to get two for the price of one. Sometimes they come and they think you have not felt it, and they try to come again. But, then, you show them (pretending to hold up a condom) and say: "What's that at the bottom, hey?"

Official records show that some cases of violence and abuse committed by East Indian men, either alone or in groups, have been reported to the police and taken to the courts. Given the reluctance of female and especially transvestite prostitutes to take their complaints to the authorities, it may be assumed that more cases of violence, abuse, and theft than the ones reported have in fact taken place.

It is perhaps also not unreasonable to assume that the preconceived notions of a prostitute who "does not like going out with them" may contribute, in some cases and to some extent, to make the encounter a negative experience, a self-fulfilling prophecy which reinforces the stereotype. The story of the electric bulb was told to me in exactly the same terms thirteen months earlier by another woman, and alluded to by a third one. It is striking enough not to need any embellishment, and the variations only occurred in the closeness of the relationship between the women who repeated the story and its victim. Since behaviour such as this could not be seen as being simply individual (thus arbitrary) because of the frequency with which it is said to occur, it is explained in cultural terms:

They're usually trained to think that their women are trash. I guess they treat all women pretty bad. (Sue)

East Indians are *cheap*; anyway, because they come from a country where it's cheap ... I think these fellows tend to be abusive with their own women. (Julie)

In another interview, Julie also explained the East Indians' behaviour through their misunderstanding of Canadian culture and frustration with it. As they see Canadian women drinking, smoking, and dressed immodestly by their standards, they assume them all to be the worst type of prostitutes, and consequently brutalize prostitutes as the only Canadian women available to them.

The Narc

Narcs, because of the nature of the activities in which they willingly participate, are be definition "assholes." "They turn my stomach" (Sugar); "The lowest" (Tiny); "Any sneaky behaviour that looks sneaky, it's a narc:" (Bugsy); "How do you know the narcs? When the door comes in!" (Bugsy); "Cops, pigs, and bulls, they're all the same; only some are worse: the narcs!" (Dee). The folk stories related to narc-street transactions are full of violence. "They hit me in the stomach and I miscarried." (Sue). The women describe incidents of "throttling" and "hassling." Instances of broken teeth or choking while searching for dope concealed in the suspect's mouth and ready to be swallowed, are said to have been frequent in the past. Nowadays, narcs are mostly accused of "playing dirty." "They frame you" (Dee, Brandy, Julie). "They go behind your back and tell your employer that you are a junkie or an ex-con and they tell him to fire you or else!" (Jo and Snow). Long, intricate stories are told to demonstrate the length to which the narcs will go to "get you." Here again, an explanation is given for the type of behaviour met among members of a certain group. The cultural explanation given for the East Indians' behaviour is now replaced by a psychological one:

You have to be sadistic to be a narc. (Bugsy)

They can't handle their job. They enjoy it. They take it on everybody on the street: everybody is dirt and must be stepped on. (Tiny)

It's a personal thing, like a personal trip. They're especially after hypes and the working girls who are also addicts. (Dee)

If East Indians are physically recognizable and visibly alien to the street, the narcs' effort to pass themselves off as street people causes anger and bitterness. They "hang around the Corner" posing as "chippy hypes" or week-end users. (Dee).

To a lesser extent, members of the Morality Squad are also part of what the folklore sees as the culture's villains. It was thought at one point that police officers could not lie and, when challenged, had to answer truthfully. In their case, "bust" stories are told which detail not only the manner in which the women were made to think the cop was a *bona fide* trick, but how he deceitfully answered the question: "Are you a cop?" (Layton 1975:197 and 1979).

The two groups of villains can be contrasted from the perspective of a street-straight opposition. Rip offs and rats are individual villains; East Indians and narcs are collectively so. Reasons that may pass as excuses are found for the first group: need and fear. Culturally and psychologically, on the other hand, the other two are simply *wrong*. All street people could, in certain circumstances, although they would probably deny it, become rip offs and rats. None of them could be an East Indian or a narc.

In the street group, the rat is the most hated of the two since he has not only transgressed the rules of solidarity but has—even linguistically—crossed the line between street and straight. In the other group, the narc's villainy is twofold: He is the cultural enemy since he devotes his efforts and time to bring about the undoing of street users and traffickers, but he too has crossed the line, in reverse this time, in his attempt to look, speak, and behave like them. In a subculture that sees as essential its differentiation from, and antagonism towards, the larger culture, the least forgivable sin is perhaps crossing boundaries for reasons of villainy.

FORMAL AND SUBTERRANEAN VALUES

The norms of street life, which are also the norms of the drug addict's life: "hedonism, thrill-seeking, lack of employment, unstable formal marriages" (Young 1971:53), are incompatible with the middle-class standards of behaviour and attitudes which are seen as representative of the larger society. More than incompatibility, they represent in fact a diametral opposition to formal values, and form what is sometimes called the *subterranean* values of society.

Young (1971:126) illustrates the contrast between subterranean and formal values (the "official values of the workaday world"):

Formal Work Values: deferred gratification
Subterranean Values: short-term hedonism

Formal Work Values: planning future action
Subterranean Values: spontaneity

Formal Work Values: conformity to bureaucratic rules
Subterranean Values: ego-expressivity

Formal Work Values: fatalism, high control over detail, little control over direction
Subterranean Values: autonomy, control of behaviour in detail and direction

Formal Work Values: routine, predictability
Subterranean Values: new experience, excitement

Formal Work Values: instrumental attitudes to work
Subterranean Values: activities performed as an end-in-themselves

Formal Work Values: hard productive work as a virtue
Subterranean Values: disdain for work

These subterranean values are only released in the straight world at intermittent, institutionalized periods (holidays, festivals, etc.); thus, the two sets of values are said to coexist in our society. In fact, these two sets of values contradict each other. Straight and Street norms are not only different: They are mutually exclusive, and their safeguard and cohesion depend on the maintenance of boundaries between the two cultures.

CHAPTER SIX

DEFINITIONS AND TRANSACTIONS

JUNKIE-PROSTITUTES, TRICKS, MARKS

This chapter provides further definitions of members of the two groups who are engaged in a relationship seen as mutually exploitative by the informants. The transactions performed achieve a balance when a prostitute's professional services are obtained and paid for, and an elementary contract is then fulfilled. Many instances occur, however, when events may cause this contract not to be fulfilled. These events (robbery, beating, arrest) may be determined by the characteristics of the trick or the woman herself.

A streetwalker's habitual soliciting technique consists mostly in stating the amount her expected remuneration in terms which would not lead to her arrest, should the potential trick be in fact a member of the Morality Squad (Layton 1979). It consists also, at times, in eliciting from a perhaps diffident customer the nature of his needs. Beyond this basic display of verbal skills, a woman may be called upon to handle problematic and difficult cases where her mastery of verbal manipulation may make the difference between a safe outcome and a violent encounter. She may find herself placed in these problematic circumstances in her role of prostitute or drug addict.

The subculture of the drug addict has been well described by a number of authors (Preble and Casey 1969, Agar 1973) who themselves comment and evaluate previous works on the subject. Stoddart (1968) has already described the drug addicts' transactions in the same city where my informants operate. Consequently, we will gloss over the various and well-known *connections* that form the trafficking network among users.

The junkie-prostitute considered here is often herself a trafficker. She is however almost exclusively a small-time connection, who sells directly on the street. Let us remember Bugsy who, in her Mafia story has the "guys from the Mafia" asking for an *ounce* (400 caps). She, herself, sells *caps,* which she obtains from a *middle man* dealing in *bundles* (25 caps), and, for her, those who deal in ounces are as far removed in the hierarchy of crime as the Mafia organization is from the petty larceny she knows. But in fact, traffickers in ounces are themselves only three or four times removed from the street sellers, and not terribly high up in this hierarchy.

It should also be pointed out that, as in many other walks of life, a woman's status may depend on her mate's. He may be a higher connection than one would normally expect *her* to be, judging from her other activities. However, she may be only *putting out* for him directly on the street, thus returning to what is seen as her proper, inferior, status. In effect, her availability on the street, her variable but secure income, and her needs (ever increasing but controlled by the need to be visible as a street walker) contribute to keep the junkie-prostitute at that particular level, the lowest, of trafficking, when trafficking is one of her means of livelihood.

Photograph courtesy of Lincoln Clarkes
(Worldwide Green Eyes)

There are a number of people marginally involved with the street, with whom the informants interact, and who will only be briefly described, such as the ironically named *teeny boppers:*

> Kids around The Corner, hanging around and trying to be a rounder. They say things like: "I drink hard likker" "I smoke dope" "Hey, man, you scored?" and then you find out that. they are talking about MDA or something like that, not stuff. They are a

nuisance to a working girl. T*hey* talk to you, "I have ten bucks, you wanna ..." (Dee and Bugsy)

Julie spoke in a derogatory manner of their "frenzied state," their overzealous interest in what goes on the street, their "loving the excitement," their irresponsibility. Not being "very, very solid in their own mind," they are a risk to street people who cannot afford to have them around.

Others are the employees of the arcades, restaurants, coffee shops, and pool rooms frequented by street people. Others, still, are people working in hotels or "rooms" who may be willing to knock on the door after half an hour and ask "Everything O.K.?" or else do not want to get involved and "don't give a shit and can't hear nothing if you scream!"

Part-timer operators such as *chippie hookers* or *chippie hypes* are also common characters. They are not really part of the street and would be overlooked if they did not in fact represent a potential danger: Undercover police officers are rumoured to pose sometimes as chippie hypes.

Fences and pawnshop operators are also part of a junkie prostitute's life: "A fence is into anything that's illegal—and they're always wondering about the illegal part of what they're buying, like serial numbers. That's all they care about ... Pretty well most of the time, fences are straight. (Julie) In contrast to the fence, the pawnshop operator is described as keeping in touch with the police who "inform them on what's hot and what's not."

All these people gravitate around street people, but this chapter will consider basically two people: the prostitute and the *trick*. Since the trick may become a *mark*, the latter will also be considered in this new role. And, since the junkie-prostitute may mistake for a trick or a buyer someone who is in fact a member of the Morality Squad or the Narcotics Squad, the role of police officers is also considered here, but only in this limited capacity.

THE PROSTITUTE

In his analysis of urban nomads, Spradley (1972b:239-240) briefly delineates the various models used in the studies of Skid Road alcoholics, showing the different group interpretations and the composite portrait they form. The same could be done for prostitutes, if only to contrast these various models with the street emic one.

The *straight model* of the prostitute, based on cultural, knowledge, appears to provide the following characteristics. She was "hooked" on drugs by a pimp so that he could gain control over her. She is sadly abused and often beaten by her pimp, while being emotionally and sexually dependent on him. She sometimes has a "heart of gold." She is mainly responsible for spreading venereal diseases. She dies in "the gutter" or, in a few cases, she may become wealthy and fade into respectable retirement. In 1972, Stoddart asked a class of first year university students to depict prostitutes: greed, lewdness, and cold-hearted frigidity were most frequently seen as their characteristic attributes, as they haunted sleazy bars in the Skid Road area. In 1975, I also found that 95 percent of the students and neighbours I interviewed believed prostitution to be illegal, therefore a criminal activity.

Photograph courtesy of Lincoln Clarkes

(Worldwide Green Eyes)

The *legal model* is an ambiguous one, since it has to recognize that prostitution, like drug addiction, is not an illegal activity. Yet, since it is, like drug addiction, a morally reprehensible one, legal control has to be achieved over its perpetrators with statutes which are difficult to endorse because—as to a lesser extent in the case of those dealing with drug possession—they recognize the legitimacy of an action while attempting

Hastings Street at the bottom. Brandy's classification is interesting in that she sees as the crucial differentiating factor among the various types of prostitutes the type of drug they use. From this alone derives the type of prostitution they either favour or can only expect to practise, with its ensuing social consequences. She explicitly described a decreasing social and occupational status following an increasing involvement with the more addictive drugs.

From the other informants, I obtained five main categories: call girls; hookers working in saunas, steam baths, and massage parlours; camp to camp hookers; hookers working in hotels, lounges, and bars; and street girls. There appears to be a certain amount of mobility among the members of the last two groups. Whereas street walkers would not work in the most expensive hotels in town, they often frequent less exclusive bars and hotel lounges. There is also a certain amount of mobility in the sense that women who work in hotels have often started, and will again end up, on the street.

1.   *Call Girls*
Dee saw them usually in their 30s, often with a trade of sadists who "know where to go" and do not want to risk unknown working girls on the street. Most of their regular customers have become marks. They are said to live usually in "an apartment in a high rise in the West End." The fees they charge were open to speculation, ranging from "probably a minimum of $100 for at least an hour" to "hundreds and even thousands of dollars." Bugsy said she "wouldn't mind being a call girl: They stay at home!" They were reputed to "have it easier" since "they don't have to worry about the cops." Beside, most of them are said to "have a legal job" as well. "Sometimes they phone, and sometimes they get phoned." Rather wistfully, Bugsy repeated: "They're inside, they're not down on the street!" She described the way she assumed one could become a call girl:

> You give your tricks your phone number and tell them you're not going to be coming downtown no more, and they'll have to phone. If they're steady tricks, they will.

Another woman reported:

> I've been in this business for a year. I'm with a girl friend, and we're making up some business cards with our phone number on it. We're going to give those out and when we're well known, we won't have to work on the street.

But Bugsy concluded: "It's very difficult to tell about call girls, 'cause I've never been a call girl." Only Boots, in fact, said she knew anything about call girls.

2.   *Massage Parlours and Steam Baths*
Much like call girls, women working in sauna baths, steam baths, and massage parlours were reputed to have it "easier" since they do not work on the street. They were thought to be "usually non addicts" and "usually with a pimp." In the 1970s, having female prostitutes in these establishments was a relatively new thing in Vancouver and my informants knew little about them. It is possible that since these women were said to be non-addicts and to operate off the street, their paths would not have crossed very often.

3.   *Camp to Camp Hookers*
They usually travel in groups of three, four, or five women, with occasionally a male or transvestite prostitute among them. They are accompanied by a pimp who "shares himself" and is white; it was thought that the loggers and construction workers who form their clientele would not accept a black pimp among them. They travel from camp to camp in the province, for about five months every year. The work is reputed to be hard, but it is also said to pay very well. "They make real good money" (Dee); "Some might be junkies, but they've kicked their habit for a while, you know, trying to save all that money." (Julie)

4.   *Bar, Hotel, and Lounge Girls*

Part time practitioners, such as chippie or weekend hookers were said to prefer operating from bars and hotels rather than work in the less protected environment of the street. Women who work in bars and hotels were said to require good clothes and good grooming. Those among them who are full-time hookers were said to be mostly non-addicts and working for a pimp. Some of them, especially weekend hookers who may work only on special occasions were said to be hired for conventions. If they specialize in that type of work, they are known as *stag girls*. "They work at parties and banquets, and probably get $200 to go there, and then they get extra payment from individual men." (Dee) My informants also stated that the women who travel from the Pacific National Exhibition (PNE) in Vancouver, to Klondike Days in the Yukon, to the Calgary Stampede, come from the ranks of the bar girls, as well as the "better" street girls.

5.   *Street Girls*

Streetwalkers were defined by Dee as "girls who work on the street, but it's hardly ever used." Dee, not herself a prostitute but with many friends who are, believed the street girls' trade to be often made of "masochists who don't like to ask their wives." Street hookers themselves said they "get all types," and will charge higher for special services. Their fees are normally $35 (East Hastings and Granville) or $50 (Granville and Davie) for twenty minutes of their time. Characteristically, the price of one trick follows the price of heroin: one cap, one trick. Most street girls were said to be hypes (addicts) who were sometimes desperate enough to lower their prices when the trade is poor, the weather bad, or the hour late.

When their appearance worsens or they get too old to frequent their ordinary places of work they may become *sleazies* or *flea bags* and "turn tricks in cheap hotels in Skid Road." They are not to be confused with "old-timers," who may in fact be quite young, but "have been at it along time and know all the tricks of the trade," and are moreover thought to be "reliable" or "solid," and can give good advice.

6   *Hookers on the boats* are often young Indian women or juvenile girls who frequent the harbour, where they are picked up and taken to the boats. They are more likely to consume alcohol than take hard drugs; they are on the whole not very highly regarded by other street girls because of their age group and racial origin. A contributing factor to this lack of regard is their choice of drug: They are perhaps the only ones still accused of sniffing glue. Their lack of professionalism is further reflected in the inconsistency of the money they command.

In 1975, I was given information on some of those young girls (not all of them prostitutes) who frequented the waterfront and the ships, suggesting that they sometimes encountered dangerous situations on board, where some were reputed to stay for as long as two or three weeks. When discovered by the Harbour Police, they were often let go with a warning, rather than be arrested for trespassing (Layton 1975:110-112)

Certain terms can refer to women who operate in different categories, but my informants usually applied them to street girls: the *chippie* hooker who works mostly as a hobby, the *turn out* who "has just started hooking," the *rip off* who is only or mostly interested in robbing her customers, finally, the *out of town* girl who is reputed to bank on the novelty she provides: "Anyone who's from out of town, she gets *all* the business, because she's new, and usually the out of town girls dress a lot nicer too."

As an aside, many of the same types were already at work in the streets of Vancouver in the early 1900s, when men from the logging camps came to town to spend their hard earned money and were a good source of income (see Appendix E about the unlucky logger). A look at the Police arrest book at the City Archives, the *Rogues Gallery,* shows our now familiar characters already practicing their trade. The *rip off:* "This woman got L. into the alley and while having connections with her she stole his money" (July 24, 1904).[14] The *hype:* "This woman is an opium

---

[14] The more picturesque name of *buttock-and-file* was given to this well-known type of practitioner in the 17th and 18th centuries in England. Cited by Kockars (1974:5), Patrick Pringle describes in *The*

fiend" (Feb. 20th, 1905). The *chippie* or *weekend hooker:* Two young women, 19 and 17 years old, were described as gainfully employed as a "laundress" and a "tailoress" (Aug. 3, 1904). *Common street walkers* or *night walkers* as they were then called, were usually more heavily penalized than the many women who resided in the numerous "houses of ill fame" on the old Dupont (now Pender) Street.

In the 1970s, my informants knew of black pimps, stables, and "main ladies," but, as a rule, they only knew them by hearsay.[15] Some believed that "the black guys around the Stratford used to carry knives or guns"; some were impressed or amused with the way they dress: "His pants were so tight, I thought he would self-destruct!" They recognized the main lady's high status: "She's a black pimp's girl; she does not have to work; she's the one he's the most fond of." Apart from Boots who reported having worked for a pimp and liked it, my informants said that they did not understand how one could be so "dumb" as to work for a pimp ("those leeches!"), and believed that the women who do have "bought the pimps' philosophy of themselves," a "philosophy" which holds the pimp as protector, lover, and business partner. Compared to James' informants and to the data coming from the Milners (1972), their knowledge was scant. Women previously met in 1975, who admitted to have worked for a very short time for a black pimp hardly appear more knowledgeable. I have no reason to suspect them of being evasive since, as drug addicts, they would not work very well in a stable system and probably did not find themselves too actively pressed into joining one.

Thief Taker the of Mary, Jonathan Wild the Great's "old lady": "Like many of her colleagues on the game, she was in the crooks' slang of that time, a buttock-and-file. The first word meant whore and the second pickpocket, and the reason for the hyphen is that she did both jobs at the same time. Most whores did their business standing in the street, and a girl with a light touch was in a good position to pick her customers' pockets when he was likely to be somewhat off his guard. The main danger is that he would discover the theft before she had time to get away, so most girls liked to have a boyfriend lurking in the shadows. He was called a twang" (p. 21).

[15] At the time, the pimps were mostly black Americans or Jamaicans, or local white men.

Sugar's description of the black and white pimps' way of running their affairs can be used as a recapitulation of all the traits mentioned by the various informants:

> There's the odd white pimp. I saw them in Prince George. They usually have 4 or 5 hookers with them. The ones I seen seemed a bit better than the black ones. Not as mean. The girls cashed in, but they were not beaten up and made to go out and work.

> A pimp takes everything, and he buys you clothes and he keeps you, and sees that you are fed and clothed. Most of them are coloured pimps. It's "Get out and make that money and get home, or else!" Some girls say the reason they work for black pimps is because they make them work. They say "I'd never go out to work if I were on my own. I'd never make any money. I'd get lazy if I did not have someone to make me work"[16] but they never see any of that money anyway!

Finally, my informants also recognized another group of prostitutes: the male *hustler,* who is sometimes a *drag queen.* Among transvestites and transsexuals, "some are working to support their habit and some are working to get their operation." Since they too solicit men, they appear to be seen as colleagues and, at times, competitors.

THE TRICK

A *trick* is a prostitute's customer. He can be a *good trick:* "He's fast, pays you good and is no trouble"[17] or he can be a *bad trick,* such as a nut, a flip, a weirdo, a pervert, and so on. Bugsy was

---

[16] Iceberg Slim, the pimp par excellence, describes this argument as the one most frequently used by pimps and eagerly accepted by the women in their stables.
[17] This definition refers to the trick as a person, whereas "Do, over with, parted, and finished" refers to the good trick as a transaction.

exceptional among my informants in that she did not express a general contempt for her customers and dislike for her work.

> Oh, I enjoy it *[being a hooker]* to an extent, but nothing more! It's not something that ... you wake up in the morning and you run out and do! I take my time doing it ... When I'm getting out, the first night, I'm going down to turn 2 tricks and score! ... and then I'm going to quit ... Then, if I turn a trick, it might be for rent, or something ... or maybe just to go and get drunk ... I don't do it for pleasure. I'd never do it if I didn't have to ...

At the other extreme, for Tiny, all tricks were "horny old bastards" and there were only two types of tricks: "He's a weirdo, or not a weirdo." For Brandy also they were all "bastards": "The only way they get their kick out of life is through a piece of tail." The very straightness of their life is what makes them what they are: "They are straight, they work all day, they have a wife and kids at home. They want to do kinky things" (Brandy). When I asked my informants to sort out words in a way that "made sense" to them, they included in the trick domain such adjectives as *flippy*, *rank*, or *ignorant*, or people such as a *jerk*, a *sucker*, or an *asshole*, who can be found among various types of tricks.

Basically, the customers were divided into "tricks to stay away from," such as *East Indians, perverts, freaks, sadists, weirdoes, drunks*, or "tricks that it's all right to go out with," such as *greenhorns, students, fast tricks, regular or steady tricks, servicemen, Greek sailors, straight tricks, old men, masochists, Orientals, talkers*.

The Good Tricks

Students: This category usually refers to students from colleges, universities, technical, or vocational schools. The younger ones are normally called *greenhorns;* they are "young guys, they don't know what they're doing." The older students

Don't usually ask for the same things as the other tricks: Most want a straight lay. Often, they do their lay and then offer you another thirty bucks to talk or take you for a drink. They like to talk about what they do in college. They say they have nobody to talk to. (Bugsy and Dee)

Fast tricks are, naturally enough, "guys who turn their trick very fast." When they do not argue that the woman owes them time, they are the ideal customer.

Regular or *steady tricks*: They "could be marks, but they're not that steady: they come about twice a week." As regular customers, they do not necessarily receive special treatment. Julie believed that it would spoil their relationship:

If you do, you're changing and he'll probably wonder why. What would be coming over you, that you're so friendly, if you are? There's no reason to treat him any better than what you've already found works.

Yet, women who have the ambition to become call girls tend to cultivate a steady trick. Moreover, as James mentions, "when times are hard, he is the bread and butter of the prostitute." (1972a:63)

Servicemen are "guys on ships and stuff." Yet, a distinct category seems to exist for the *Greek sailors* who take on board the waterfront women and girls (Layton 1975:110-112). Servicemen are more likely to pick up the women on the street or in bars.

Straight tricks: They are straight Johns wanting a "straight lay."

Old men: Opinions about them vary from Brandy who referred to them as "perverted old bastards" to Bugsy who liked them. They are however classified as "good tricks" by all.

Masochists: These are reputed to be "straight guys, square Johns who are too embarrassed or afraid to ask their wives." Dee also believed that "the girls like to go out with them: They take their frustrations out on the poor guys!" Sugar confirmed this view: "He's all right. We do it to *them.* They like pain!" Tiny saw a danger for the prostitutes who become "involved in that S. & M. They enjoy it. Those who enjoy it are a bigger trick. It's a weakness, because it is not business anymore."

Orientals: In Vancouver, the Orientals are all Chinese. "They're cheap and easy!" (Dee). "They're fast, so that's good. From what I gather, they don't pay well ... Most of them are really cheap ... But it's just five minutes and you're on the street again!" (Sue)

Talkers: Talkers are tricks who "want mostly conversation." It is safe to go out with them but, unfortunately, "they take lots more time," (Dee) and many women resented this.

The Bad Tricks

The preceding chapter mentions the collective reputation acquired by East Indians. Other villains are *freaks,* who may also be known as sadists.

> He can be crazy: He's liable to freak out on you, and he's more likely to hurt you than a pervert. (Sugar)

> They hate whores. They threaten girls with a knife or a revolver. The best is to fight back: If you cower, they'll get worse. (Brandy)

Many women, on the contrary, thought it was wiser and safer to "play it cool" (see next section in this chapter). It was believed that there may be less danger from freaks now than in the past: more women are carrying knives and there is more police protection. Unfortunately, evidence does not always support this conceit.

Some women put *weirdos* in a separate category. A weirdo said Sugar, is

Weird in the way he looks, weird in what he likes, about his sex ideas, but he's not necessarily dangerous. Some guys like to see you pee in a glass or they want you to pee on their face. They're good tricks because they're fast.

Yet, most women were leery of them since there is always a possibility that mood might abruptly change.

Perverts are very much like weirdos. They, like weirdos, are not as likely to hurt women as freaks. A pervert, explained Sugar,

Can have different things that he likes with sex: for instance, he can get off on watching two girls together, or he can be a peeping Tom. He's not necessarily going to hurt you.

Drunks are more ambivalent tricks. They are easy to rip off and, for that reason, some women preferred them and considered themselves very good at handling them. Jo, for instance, talked them to sleep. Many others, however, found them *flippy*. They are mostly annoying because:

It takes a lot of time and a lot of energy. Sometime they have not even come after an hour, and they keep on saying that they'll come in a minute! (Bugsy)

Watch out for them! They can't get off. (Sugar)

Experience and intuition, once more, will help decide whether a drunk will be a good or a bad trick:

You can get more money out of them, but you've got to be on your guard. You can usually tell if he's obnoxious or ignorant. (Sugar)

They vary. Some of them get nasty, some of them don't. The girls get where they can sort of judge just by talking to the guy.(Sue)

Tricks, good or bad, are the means of livelihood of non-addict streetwalkers. And although female addicts often have other ways to make a living, prostitution remains as a rule the most profitable one.

TRANSACTIONS

The various transactions between prostitutes and their customers usually start on the street where contact is made and a preliminary contract is drawn. The relationship between prostitutes and their customers may be seen as the most complex one on the street, since the main characteristics of the two groups are diametrically opposed: *male-female, buyer-seller, straight-street, non user-addict*. Yet, the first two pairs of opposites are also complementary, and many women argue that the tricks' curiosity or perversity makes it equally true of the second pair. This divergent-convergent relationship of the two groups is not its only paradox since, just as paradoxically, this mutually exploitative relationship is also based on mutual trust.

The mutual exploitation - where the woman often attempts to talk herself into performing as few sexual services as possible or even out of performing any, and where the man is often said to feel that he is "buying" the person as much as the services—this mutual exploitation, however, can only take place once the basic premise of *trust* has been established. In his study of the relationship between cab drivers and fares (one which can also be problematic at times), Henslin (1968:141) draws a list of criteria to be met by drivers and fares before trust could be established. These criteria are singularly similar to those that could be drawn between prostitutes and their customers before trust could be established between them.

Under optimum circumstances, both driver and prostitute (1) offer a service that they are both willing and able to provide; (2) appear to be able to provide an exchange for services that are defined as being at least equal to, or more than, the service was worth under the circumstances; (3) appear as if they will in fact provide such an exchange; and (4) offer to provide an exchange that represents little or no risk to themselves. Similarly, the fare or the trick must also trust the driver or the prostitute to be only what they appear to be, and assume that the service will be performed and that they will not be robbed or manhandled.

The initial transactions which commonly take place between prostitutes and their customers may lead to different outcomes. An initial contract is usually drawn on the street between the two. It normally defines the type of services to be performed, the time to be spent, and the price to be paid. Both parties having agreed upon the terms of this simple contract will then retire to a room. The customer pays the agreed upon price before the services are performed. This transaction (#1) is the one usually known as a "good trick," where the word "trick" refers to both the customer and to the transaction itself.

Contract—payment—performance

Situation 1

There are, however, many other possibilities stemming from the initial contract. Some women, for instance, have indicated that a customer's shyness may sometimes prevent him from expressing at the beginning what he really wants, but once this reluctance is overcome, perhaps later when they have already "gone up," a new price may then be agreed upon and paid beforehand; or the newly defined transaction may be rejected by the woman. The customer may then respect her wishes and agree to have the contract annulled. On the other hand, the customer may not accept her refusal and violates the annulment. This violation is often accompanied by violence. He may either pay her afterwards, or refuse to pay her, thus robbing her of the money earned under stress, or even rob her of whatever money she already had in her possession as a further "punishment" (#2).

Contract—new request:

(a) *agreement* : new contract—new payment—performance

(b) *agreement* : cancellation of contract

(c) *disagreement*: (i) violation—performance—payment

(ii) violation—performance— no payment

(iii) violation—performance—no payment—robbery

Situation 2

The same situation may also occur after the initial contract has been fulfilled. A further request may be made (#3) with a pattern similar to the previous one.

Contract —payment—performance—new request:

(a) *agreement* : (i)newcontract—new payment—performance

(b) agreement : (ii) no new contract— no payment—no performance

(c) disagreement: (i) violation—performance—new payment

(ii) violation—performance— no payment

(iii) violation—performance—no payment—robbery

Situation 3

In other cases, a customer may simply refuse to pay the woman after they have agreed to "go up," but demand that she fulfill her part of the contract, and may further rob her. (#4)

contract – *disagreement* : (i) violation—non-payment

(ii) violation—performance—non payment—robbery

Situation 4

Or, again, a customer may first pay the prostitute to ensure satisfactory services, then later demand that she return his money, or even any other money she may already have in her possession. The woman may or may not willingly comply (#5)

Contract: payment—performance—cancellation of contract

    (a) *agreement*: performance—robbery

    (b) *disagreement*: violation—performance— robbery

Situation 5

Or, finally, the "customer" may turn out to be an officer of the Morality Squad (#6).

Contract—no payment—no performance—arrest

Situation 6

These are, essentially, the six possible situations which may result from the initial contract. In the short time allowed for the preliminary interaction, the woman has to read the various cues which will enable her to assess the type of transaction she is facing.

Henslin (1968), as a cab driver, was able to pinpoint the cues on which he based his evaluation of potential fares and established his trust. In spite of my informants' good will, I found it difficult to determine the rules of character evaluation which help street women trust on sight a good trick ("He's fast, he pays you good, and he's no trouble," (Sugar)), mistrust a freak or a pervert, or suspect a cop.

They claim that a woman usually trusts what she may call her "intuition." (Snow) The man's physical appearance and his manner of speaking serve to provide clues. Jo and Snow explained:

> - If the guy's a flip, you won't know it. You can't   usually tell.
> - I always go by feeling. Like, a guy who's really nervous or something, I won't go. Or if he looks weird, you know?
> - With his hair long...
> - And he's grubby, or the way he talks, the way he acts. I'll talk for a few minutes in the street, you know, to sort of getting an idea, you know. Then, I'll go, only then.

Brandy and I discussed the case, reported in the newspapers, of a woman who had been severely beaten by a paraplegic customer. She concluded: "I'd never go with someone that would have an arm or a leg missing, or something like that. They would be bound to have real hang ups." Yet, several months earlier, she had confidently described men with an obvious disability as usually "pretty straight and meek," even adding that prostitute sometimes tried to build up their self-confidence.

A cop or a pervert propose two different types of transactions. Whereas one might simply get a "feeling" (Tiny, Sugar, Brandy, Snow) about them, experience would perhaps dictate whether the "bad vibes" (Sugar) received were sent off by a police officer or a sadistic customer. This does not seem to be the case however. When I asked Bugsy why she had turned down one particular customer, she suggested that he could easily have been either: "I don't know why ... I didn't like him ... I probably thought he was a cop, and I didn't like his looks, anyways. He looked like one wrong move and the game's over!" In fact, he turned out to be a particularly "good trick," as her girl friend later reported.

A policeman's physical appearance does not necessarily give him away, but certain restrictions, such as size, age, weight, physical disabilities, would prevent a man from being on the Police Force. These serve as clues. Policemen also follow a certain routine when they are about to arrest a prostitute, which give away their intentions, unfortunately too late for the woman.

> I says: "How much will you spend?" He says: "Fifty bucks."
> I says: "O.K." He says: "Just a second, I want to park my car." I says: "Yeah!" and *I knew* he was a cop! Why? Just by what he said! And then he left and he did not come back *[the arrest was performed by another officer]*. It was the way he acted. And then, it dawned on me ... Like, I was sick *this explains why her alertness was somewhat reduced]*. And then it dawned on me that I'd never seen him before ... and he just comes up, like: "I've got to park my car! (Bugsy)

A friend of Bugsy's had a much more tangible clue to assist her:

> When she was going up, she realized he was a cop, and she'd
> solicited him! She realized he was a cop 'cause she'd seen
> his handcuffs!

Descriptions of undercover police officers are circulated among streetwalkers; others are simply recognized and the word is passed around.

In the same manner, bad tricks are also talked about and described. *Car tricks* are often avoided; many women refuse to get into a customer's car; others mention taking down the license number before getting into it. A good many women carry a knife on them and say that they are ready to use it to protect themselves. For, in spite of their "intuition" and their "feeling", they agree that "you can never tell whether a guy is a nut or not. They may just turn on you, like that, for no reason." (Dee)

Everything was O.K. and when we had finished, I says: "I'm gonna leave." I was getting dressed and when I turned around, he cracked me on the head with a candlestick holder. He was a nut! He wanted more, and everything, and he wasn't planning to let me go! (Bugsy)

This is a case similar to transaction #3, but Bugsy was not even given the chance to agree with him.

If the prostitute takes a chance every time she agrees to go with a customer, she is also willing to admit that he too may be taking a chance.

Like, one time, I was with a guy and he was going to give me 200 dollars for an hour. That was up North. And he was going to give me a hundred then and a hundred later, before I left. I said: "No way! Can't do that. You know, I'll be nervous thinking you won't pay me." So finally he just gave me all the money, but he had to go to a stash to get the rest, because he only had 100 dollars on him.. And I seen all the money and I just ... Well, I just had to have it! Before I left! I get like that. And I just ... He put it in his pocket and he was playing with television. I poured myself a drink, pulled out my knife, drank the drink, walked over and just cut money and pocket right out of his pants. How, I had to fight with him to get out of the room, but he was a lot older than I was, so it wasn't too much trouble. (Jo)

Julie, who prides herself on the efficacy of her manipulative techniques, does it in another way:

You pick up a trick and you go with him to his hotel room, and during the course of whatever may be happening or turning out, there's always the opportunity to snap at his wallet ... And he's always got his back turned at one time! You know, he's not always staring at you ... And you can play the little girl act, you know: "You don't trust me?" So, he just thinks: "Oh, God! The poor little thing is just going to *shrivel* up if I don't trust her!" So he'll finally go to the washroom, maybe even shut the door, and you've got a good chance! You can make maybe 180-200 dollars, you know?

Another type of encounter familiar to my informants, whether junkies or prostitutes, is the one where "intuition" has failed them and they must now resort to "coolness." When I asked Brandy what advice she would give a young girl starting out on the street, she answered: "Be cool, be careful, and ask a lot of questions." The last part of the advice may not necessarily meet with everyone's agreement, since one is always somewhat suspicious of people who ask too many questions. But the injunction to "be cool" is one with which everyone would agree.

Coolness, "poise under pressure," is defined by Lyman and Scott (1968:92) as

> The capacity to execute physical acts, including conversation, in a concerted, smooth, self-controlled fashion in risky situations, or to maintain affective detachment during the course of encounters involving considerable emotion.

Although coolness shows a certain elegance when practised in everyday life, its functions is not exclusively esthetic: Its main purpose is to get one out of dangerous situations. For the female addict, these situations usually involve a "narc" or a "pervert." The examples of the former abound, since my informants were always pleased to relate how they con people, especially police officers.

> A few times, you know, they go to throttle you, and I've got it in my mouth all the time, and I can bluff my way out of it. I say "Why, I don't have anything.'" You know, they

usually stick the handcuffs and dig for it. And they haven't done it because they figure: "Oh, she's too casual. She doesn't have any." I've had 25, 50, 75 that I've had to swallow!   (Sue)

From Julie, while "on escape":

I was sitting with some fellows from halfway house out from the B.C. Pen. These guys, I started sitting with them, drinking. I seen the police, I thought: "Oh, shit:" Now, I grabbed all the coins on the table and I went to the juke box to start feeding them in and start playing all the buttons, but I could see the reflection coming... So, they come right at me and they said: "Are you a user?" And I says: "Hell, no! I'm an alcoholic. I'm drinking here on my work hour... you know, while I'm out for lunch." And he said: "Well," he said, "you know who you're sitting with?" I said: "A bunch of guys ..." "Well," he says, "these guys are rip offs!" I said "Oh?" He says: "Yeah, they're addicts, they'll rip you off, they'll steal your money, and it'll be to your best advantage just to get the hell out of here, because they'll kill you!" "They'll be killing me?" I says, "No kidding? These can't be the guys we're talking about. These guys are nice." Meanwhile, I know my picture is flashed all over the place, and I never showed them any I.D. because they never asked for them!

Photograph courtesy of Lincoln Clarkes

(Worldwide Green Eyes)

I get the handcuffs on me, like this. There's one cop on this side of me, and one on this side of me. And when this one here, in front of me, is writing, the other one, over here, is watching. And when *he's* writing, *this* one is watching me. And I'm sitting like this, all charm, trying to get in my bra and get those two caps outta there, because they're going to take me upstairs and skin me. So this cop says: "Now," he says, "what are you gonna do?" I says *[sarcastically]*: "Now, I'm gonna go out and make more money so I can fix!" So he says: "Well ... You have nothing else on you, hey?" I says: "Do you think I'd be *dumb* enough to be sitting here if I did?" (Bugsy)

On my escape, I see the police all the time, but I wouldn't ... Like if they'd come right toward me, right? I know they'd stop me and ask my I.D., which I had my cousin's I.D., not my own. I know they would stop me, right? I thought "I'll turn around! ... No, I'll just remain calm, cool..." You know, I could turn around fast and they would stop me and ask why. So I walked by. I knew they would stop me, and he said: "Hey." And I said: "Yes?" You know, playing like I've never ... you know...(Snow)

I found it uncomfortable to question my informants on the way they kept "cool" while facing a freak, since the experience often meant that they had to obey his commands while trying to talk reasonably to him and calm him down. "The gun's pointed at me, what am I going to do? I agree ... I have to agree to everything he's going to say for me to do.

However, the transcripts of rape trials usually show the women complying with their oppressor and often abductor, while attempting to appear as natural as possible under the circumstances, i.e. unafraid but also unchallenging in order not to excite him further.

I don't remember too much of the conversation. I do remember I was saying things, trying to calm him and trying to get myself out of the situation I was in. But as to what I said and what ... I can't remember ... I did not know how I was supposed to react and I stayed calm. I didn't know what to do. I was shocked ... He kept the gun at my temple until I said to him: "Is it necessary to hold it at my head? Please, take it away. I'm cooperating with you and I won't do anything to harm you or deter you." He took it away from my head and then put it in the middle between my back and held it on my back the entire time. (Rape trial. *The plaintiff was the woman who told me in 1975 that she "wouldn't say anything important."*)

The transactions described are seen as absolutely exploitative ones. But relationships between the two groups, while not relinquishing altogether their basic nature, can be somewhat more positive than that. One informant described the roles of inmates and prison staff members: "My job is to con them. Their job is to bust me." Consequently, she does not, for instance, "ask for" a pass, but she "cons them out of" a pass. She explained that the reason she would truthfully have to give for wanting one—the need for "a good fuck"—would not be acceptable. So, she has to make up another reason that she knows will meet with the authorities' approval. On the other hand, she also admitted that "you can't pull one over" the staff member in charge of granting passes. Actually, the whole exchange was viewed as much in terms of showing "respect" as in terms of "conning." The same woman gave several examples where the staff were either "respected" or "disrespected" in their authority. Such an example related to the wearing of shoes. Inmates are not supposed to wear their own shoes. However, many do. And they show their "respect" by allowing their pant legs to cover these shoes, thus not flaunting their disobedience. "Disrespect" would consist in making this disobedience obvious to a matron, forcing her to take action.

The same relationship is extended on the street to other members of what some informants classified for me as the "Authorities": police, judiciary, etc. *Conning-busting* is seen as the essential complementary relationship, tempered however with the notion of *respect-disrespect.*

Thus, in this sense, the use of "respect" (i.e. the respect for the other's rights and duties) is an intrinsic component of the conning behaviour. By not forcing the issue, the manipulative individual has conned the other one in accepting the status quo (a similar technique is often used in marriages where the dominant role of one mate is traditionally recognized. (Anderson 1974:62-63) The street version of this situation is the blind eye turned by policemen on the activities of a prostitute who tries to operate with discretion.

The notion of respect (this time without its implicit value as a manipulative tool) is often mentioned as a significant factor in positive straight-street relationships. Brandy could not accept the authority of "young kids, just out of university" who tell her what to do, but "respects" her present probation officer, "an ex-con who's been there." After three months of frequent talks with Bugsy, when it became clear to her that I really liked her, she said: "I wouldn't mind having you as my probation officer." This was obviously the highest compliment she could have paid me, one which also envisaged a reasonable and realistic continuation of a relationship between us, set in a context more familiar to her than the present one. It also established without any doubt that, as close as we could ever become, she did not conceive—even in the passing warmth of a fleeting moment of benevolence—that we could ever cross the dividing line between our respective cultures. A further explanation, one I was a little reluctant to consider, was that she saw me as someone easy to con.

THE MARK

The con man's mark and the women's mark have so far been considered here as one and the same individual. However, an interesting difference exists between the two. The mark who is victim of a con man is "the sucker—the person who is taken in." (Goffman 1952:451) A situation is misrepresented to him and he accepts the misrepresentation as true, hoping to draw profit from it. He is later made to face the evidence of his foolishness and gullibility and must be "cooled out" in order to face and accept his loss of money and, more importantly, his loss of role. (Goffman 1952) The characters *con man* and *mark* are clear cut and the "trick" is never mistaken for the "trickster." A woman's mark, on the other hand, is a much more ambiguous character. Many women describe his as a "masochist," who will "take anything," who "knows that he's being used." (Dee) He may be "someone who's good to you and you don't have to give him anything." (Brandy)

> Some like to be treated mean. Some enjoy being hurt. They can enjoy it, sit back and say "Poor me!" I abuse them. All they get is the pleasure of being around. (Julie)

Unlike the other mark, this one appears to be getting what he wants. The usual cooling out of the mark described by Goffman would be inappropriate in this case. As with the previous mark, the relationship must be severed when the mark has run out of funds and his usefulness has ceased. But since this particular mark is, in fact, a satisfied customer —one who may possibly be reinstated at a later date—he must be treated in a different manner.

The purpose of cooling the mark out is to allow him to get over the episode. Julie's technique for leaving a mark has the opposite result. By putting him in the wrong, she keeps him in reserve.

> If I bleed him of his money, well then, it's time to go! "It's been nice!" You usually blame it on them. If you know the money's run out, then you do something to make to look like it's *their* fault you're leaving. You can always start a fight, or you can say that he'd been downtown and dropped your name to another girl, or that a girl phoned you, one of your girlfriends, and said he'd come to her. (You just don't go to somebody else

for business, right?). So, you blame him for that. Or you say a girl phoned up, you know, one of your girlfriends, and said that he had left a number with her. Now, you just lay it on him! "You just don't give a number, especially, you know, when I'm at the other end of it.'" And that's a good start for a fight. He also feels guilty, 'cause no doubt chances are that he has dropped a number once before and may be he thinks you know her. And the fight's on! And he's really *ashamed!* He feels guilty, you know. He thinks: "Oh well, shit! I must have done something ..." And, Jesus, sure he don't want' you to go, right? So, as you're packing your bags,' he's crying. So, you say that you're going to think about it. And you're not gonna let him see you for a couple of months. Or, else: "Come and see me in about a month!" So, by then, he's gathered up his money again. He'll keep bugging you. But you just tell him: "I'll talk to you as soon as I've given it some thought."

For the mark, writes Goffman (1952:456),

> Cooling represents a process of adjustment to an impossible situation—a situation arising from having defined himself in a way which the social facts come to contradict. The mark must therefore be supplied with a new set of apologies for himself, a new framework in which to see himself and judge himself.

The woman's mark need not face a situation in which facts contradict his self-image. He may indeed never know for sure that the situation was other than the way he perceived it.

The verbal manipulative skills we have described throughout, aimed at guessing the mark's needs, discarding him and possibly keeping him in reserve, evaluating a trick's intentions, keeping her cool in a dangerous confrontation, all rest on the woman's definitions of herself and of the people with whom she interacts, as well as her understanding of their characteristics.

CHAPTER SEVEN

FAILURE AND SUCCESS ON THE STREET

In the retelling of events, informants not only describe but also interpret. They establish links between what they see as causes and what they understand to be consequences. Nowhere perhaps is there a more contrasted position between Street and Straight than in the understanding of what constitutes street women's *failure* and *success.* The following brief discussion on the concepts of failure and success touches again on the subject of emics and etics and the opposite orientation of street and straight people on a topic essential to the survival of a group: the self-esteem of its members.

The informants, incarcerated female heroin addicts and prostitutes, are drawn from a group described to me by a senior probation officer as "the losers of the losers." Probation officers and counsellors often stress these women's "low self-esteem." For them, the women involved are "losers" since they have "failed" to come to terms with the conventional values of the larger society. They are moreover twice losers since they have failed to do well in their own subculture and, as a result, have been imprisoned. The high rate of recidivism among these women only confirms the labeling, a labeling already well established by the officers' training. People professionally involved with these women tend to see them as social failures. They naturally enough endorse the so-called *correctional* view point which sees them as moral failures as well, and "violators of cherished and widely shared standards of conduct and morality." (Matza 1969:15)

I adopted another perspective and, instead of discussing what outsiders see as failures, the informants and I talked about what insiders see as successes. Not only did we talk of their successes, but also of the skills that made these successes possible. The shift of emphasis from failure to success no doubt gave me an equally distorted image. I do not deny that the reported lack of self-confidence and self-esteem of hookers and junkies exist. The fresh and old slash scars on their forearms and wrists are proof enough that the stories dealing with triumphant trickery, "dynamite" junk, and good times which I collected are but one part of their life. Moreover, studies quoted by Kaplan (1975:24-26) report that subjects with low self-regard are more likely to display "the relatively specific defensive behaviors of rationalizing and projecting" (1975:21) than subjects with high self-regard. But at the time of initial and even later contact, low self-regard was not evident. The women displayed during our interviews an apparently unshakable confidence in their talents as "talkers" and connivers. And it is that repeatedly expressed self-confidence which is considered here. Behind prison walls, they enjoyed delving into past pleasures, clever cons, and generous marks. Even the rip offs, the rats, and the perverts—because they belong outside—lost some of their ominous aura. Carried away by the mood, they all promised themselves an immediate return to their way of life. "First thing I do when I get out? Score!"

I wonder to what extent the necessity of reaffirming in the course of our interviews the cultural parameters of the Street did not contribute to their self-esteem. They became "together" again, seemingly regaining this self-esteem which Becker describes as "the glow of certainty that the world of meaning is intact, that the multitude of symbols forming the self are real." (Becker 1962:85) And I also wonder to what extent the conflict between the reaffirmed values of that culture and their present incarceration, where these values are formally challenged and opposed, did not also contribute to their loss of self-esteem, again described by Becker as "the warm inner feeling of self righteousness that arms the individual against anxiety." (1962:79).

Bruce Jackson would probably apply to my informants the terms in which he describes his, and with which many of the correctional staff would likely agree:

> They represent the population that gets itself caught. With rare exceptions people do not go to jail because they are guilty of something: they go to jail because they are too dumb or broke or clumsy or unlucky to stay out. And a few happen to like it there.
>
> The people in this book have worked at a variety of occupations, all for money: turning tricks, dealing dope, heisting banks, (...) writing cheques, negotiating major or minor swindles, peddling hot merchandise and cold women. They are people who aren't criminals so much as fuckups. A lot of fuckups are in prison. (Jackson 1974: 3-4)

The main difference between the terms "losers of the losers" and "fuckups" is that one is used by square Johns and the other usually is not. The first one is patronizing and definitive, and moreover street-unacceptable because it expresses the views of a group which carries no weight on the street, a group indifferent, curious, or hostile, but normally seen as unknowledgeable. I do not think that the second term is any less patronizing, but it leaves a way out: To be a broke and unlucky fuckup does not necessarily mean that one is a loser. Even a dumb and clumsy fuckup, since it could be taken in a situational context and explain why they are presently in jail. Indeed, informants usually explained that they had been arrested because someone "had ratted on them," because they "were framed," because the police "lied and cheated," because the "narcs were going to get them anyways."

The Street provides a psychological "sanctuary" where

> Public fictions support a system of values which together with the value system of society at large, make for a world of ambivalence, contradiction and paradox, where failures are rationalized into phantom successes and weaknesses magically transformed into strengths. (Liebow 1966:214)

The negative effects of possessing disvalued attributes and behaving in disvalued ways (Kaplan 1975:42) which strongly contribute to low self-esteem can be successfully countered by rejecting society's normative expectations of one's behaviour. The former "deviant" is then accepted into a new group whose expectations he can now fulfill.

> He ceases to be considered a member of the former group and comes to be viewed as a member of the latter group; and his behaviour that violates the standards of the former membership group is no longer characterized as deviant but rather is perceived as conforming to the standards of his new membership group (Kaplan 1975:4).

Thus, in terms of what reportedly matters to the street: freedom, money, and excitement, street people are successful. In terms of what is supposed to matter the most to the straight world: a need for security in its many guises, they certainly are not successful, and neither do they seem to care. Whether street values have been rationalized to fit the failure to live by former straight values, it appears that these street values do exist, and people believe in them. It also appears that straight values are denied to the extent that success according to them is not seen as success at all. The reverse is also true and straight people even seem to go further: Not only do they deny that success exists in terms others than their own, but they sometimes go as far as calling it failure. Yet, street success, according to the contradictory street values, is seen as very real.

> The 'righteous dope fiend' has mastered the art of 'hustling'; his world is fused with the same success

symbols prevalent in conventional society. He selects a retreatist role adaptation only if he takes the social role of an 'ex-dope fiend,' or a 'sick addict.' The 'righteous dope fiend', if he retreats at all, becomes a retreatist when he quits using drugs, not when he starts using drugs. (Sutter 1966:177)

With uncharacteristic heat, Dee exclaimed, trying to overcome politely her distaste as I described what I perceive to be my way of life: "I can't understand how somebody can live like that! I can't understand how they can! I guess it's subconscious... I can't see somebody doing it!" What I saw as my strengths, for instance, were only seen as rationalized weaknesses by my informants who were, I am sure, convinced that I would never make it on the street, where people are really put to the test. This is part of the game they played with me, and the reverse may well be part of the formalized game we, the straight people, play with them.

It may well be that the basic divergence of views between straight and street people is whether the latter's "fuckup" status is seen as *permanently dispositional* or *temporarily situational.* Jones and Nisbett's study of actors and observers' divergent perceptions of the causes of behaviour would indicate that straight people, as observers of street people's actions, process information available to both groups differently from the way street people do.

> The actor's view of his behavior emphasizes the role of environmental conditions at the moment of action. The observer's view emphasizes the causal role of stable dispositional properties of the actor. We wish to argue that *there is a pervasive tendency for actors to attribute their actions to requirements, whereas observers tend to attribute the same actions to stable personal dispositions.* `This tendency often stems in part from the actor's need to justify blameworthy actions, but may also reflect a variety of other factors having nothing do

to with the maintenance of self-esteem. (Jones and Nisbett 1971:2)

The observer's focus is the actor's behaviour, rather than the environment which, from his point of view is "stable and contextual" (1971:7). The actor's focus, on the other hand, is more likely to be on "environmental cues that evoke and shape" his behaviour. (1971:7) Jones and Nisbett make the double point that different information is available to observers and actors, but when the same information is available to both, it is differently processed by them. This is a point which has already been mentioned when discussing the problem of the emic and etic perspectives.

In the case under study, my street informant (as retrospective actors) provide a different interpretation of events from the one which (as observers) we might be tempted to infer from the actions and transactions observed or, in the present case, described. The failures of street people, as my informants seem to perceive them, are situational. They are temporary failures of competence: they went out with a pervert, they got busted and sent to jail, they sold to a narc, or they got ripped off. Moreover, they often add that they had a peculiar "feeling," but being "sick" (in need of a *fix)* at the time, they threw caution to the wind. These failures are not usually rationalized into successes and can, as failures, simply be chalked up to experience.

The only negative experience which they may reluctantly see as having some positive side is imprisonment. Heroin is a pain killer and most women discover while they are in jail that they are suffering from a wide variety of ailments. The women also eat well and regularly (usually too much and complain about gaining weight, especially those about to be released) and regain their strength and their health. The rundown women who are admitted are usually released after a few months in reasonably good physical condition. To this extent, the inevitability of having to serve a prison term may be perceived as a somewhat beneficial experience. This may be the only benefit they believe they draw from it, apart from seeing a term in jail as a confirmation of their proper insiders' status. The subdued women who promise somewhat dubiously that they will "smarten up," "kick their habit," "go straight," are probably only providing the expected response to counselling and "lecturing." Experience, however, often shows that jail is a place where one recovers one's powers and from which one can once more spring into the street with renewed strength and, often, having learned a thing or two there.

Believing that, as prostitutes, they encounter contempt and curiosity, and that straight women, in particular, see their occupation as despicable, the informants first assert the basic equality of all women as prostitutes. Having thus threatened the self-esteem of straight women, they further assert their own self-esteem by describing their own transactions in terms of power gained over marks and of success.

As they describe their relationships with marks in terms of the power they hold over them, they also mention the tricks' own need for power. One of Millett's very articulate informants explained:

> What they're buying, in a way, is power. You're supposed to please them. They can tell you what to do and you're supposed to please them, follow orders themselves, you're still following *his* orders to give him orders (Millett 1971:52-53).

Yet, the final word remains hers: "I did not feel that controlled by the customer. I felt I was the boss because I could say no to the deal." (1971:53) Among my informants, Julie, in particular, was quite explicit about the part played by power in the relationship between a woman and her mark. Since she assumes, like many other informants, that marks are partly, if not mostly, masochists, this is the way she understands their needs for this type of relationship:

> Jerks have had it pretty good all their life. It's a big change, you know, for somebody who's just come

through high school with no sweat, maybe been a scholar in some athlete field, and joined in Daddy's business and Mom's business, or even done it on their own. And within a couple of years, they're sitting behind the top desk. Now, most of these people have people climbing all over them and asking questions.

In the total reversal of roles they seek, they let the woman "play with them." "Well, what am I doing now?" They're asking the questions, and you're the one that's setting all the answers up for them! "(Julie)

The more power the *jerks* have outside their relationship with a woman, the more power the woman attributes to herself within this particular relationship. This power is a vindication of her deviant status meted out by the people she now dominates. She is also vindicated against straight women's contempt by asserting the social value of prostitution:

1.   By taking in charge, willingly or unwillingly, all the nuts, flips, perverts, freaks, and sadists, she makes the streets *safer* for other women.
2.   By enabling husbands to act out fantasies or practise perversions, she often *saves* their marriage.
3.   Since, however, some customers only require a little variety, she may also *save* a marriage by advising open mindedness to straight wives:

Before I left, I had a long talk with her, and I told her: "Read that 'Hundred and One Positions'. It'll do you a lot of good." And I says: "Try some of the positions," I says, "you could be happily married and he wouldn't have to come down here looking for girls." (Bugsy)

If the women's descriptions of events tend to stress their personal successful handling of transactions, they must also stress the exceptional quality of their failures. Both serve to preserve the informants' self-esteem. Reasons for accounting for what the outsider-observer might take as errors of judgement or lack of competence (i.e. decisions leading to an arrest, a rip off, or a beating) all give the context of an *exceptional* situation, an *accidental* lapse of one's *customary* competence, or an *unusual* set of circumstances.

In other cases, the situation was *unavoidable* and no one, in spite of their competence or alertness, could have foreseen it, except as a constant possibility. This is the case of the *nut,* for instance. Everyone concurs that "you can't tell a nut." Bugsy stressed that fact when she pointed out in one of her stories that "everything was O.K." and they even had "finished" and her customer had acted normally, until he suddenly "cracked" her on the head. The logic of the situation was then violated and no one could have done better than Bugsy in the same circumstances. The rule of the impredictability of the nut or the *flip,* is so well established that Bugsy can even build up in a comic vein the reverse story of the impredictability of the good trick (Chapter Five). Equally unavoidable, and also *unfair,* is the situation in which one is "tricked" by a narc playing "dirty" ("lying and cheating").

In other cases, failure to evaluate properly available information or clues can also be blamed on an unusual and *understandable* (and perhaps even *excusable)* carelessness:

> Sometimes they aren't as careful as usual. A guy might
> be sick himself and want to get rid of the last few caps
> and get out so he can fix. Or he might think you "look"
> okay. That's how come they get caught, though
> (Stoddart 1968:76).

Thus Bugsy once explained that her usual alertness had failed her and she solicited a police officer because she was "sick."

Furthermore, as Stoddart points out (1968:107), when arrest is defined as "normal," failure to be arrested may be taken as evidence of abnormality. One may even be encouraged to think of arrest (a failure by straight standards) as a "successful" attempt at showing one's legitimate status in the community.

Bugsy was adamant that a woman we both knew must have been a police informer since she had never been arrested—which, by the way, was untrue since I knew the woman had a police record. This widely held belief explains the concern shown by one of Stoddart's informants, especially at a time when stricter control followed the easy-going early days: "If I don't get pinched soon, people are gonna start gettin' suspicious of me. They'll figure I'm a fink or something." (1968:108)

When Stoddart wrote in the 1960s, it could be said that

> If you use junk, you're gonna get pinched. That's all there is to it. It may take them a while to catch on to you, but sooner or later you'll get it. The only people that don't get pinched are the finks, the guys that are keepin' out by workin' with the bulls (1968:107).

Ten years later, when I covered the same material, this belief has only been strengthened. It provides a further excuse for shifting the burden of responsibility from the victim to an outside cause and denies the reason of the individual's incompetence.

Whatever the reasons for one's failures, they seldom reflect a basic incompetence on the part of the individual. In ordinary circumstances, competent behaviour is assumed to be exercised as a matter of course, and reasonable and foreseeable problems are competently handled. The ones that have not been met successfully are usually made to appear (in their retelling at least) such that *normal competence* alone is not enough to deal with them in a satisfactory manner.

CHAPTER EIGHT

VERBAL SKILLS, MANAGEMENT,

AND CULTURAL CONTEXT

The informants' self-perceived manipulations of outsiders only form one aspect of the oral culture of the group. The didactic use of anecdotes, gossip, jokes, tales, on the one hand, and the definition of a common linguistic framework firmly excluding outsiders on the other, are characteristic of groups which rely predominantly on their oral culture to perpetuate their values and strengthen their boundaries. Although these have also been described, the study's emphasis is on the skills of verbal manipulation because, as an object of cultural pride, it reflects the group's self-perception and self-definition.

Verbal manipulative techniques such as the ones described by my informants are seen as essential to their survival. They see themselves constantly threatened as *prostitutes* (by rip offs, bad tricks, Morality Squad detectives, straight women's contempt), as *drug_addicts* (by rip offs, narcs, lack of drugs), as *jail inmates* (by the prison structure and regulations, by individual staff members, by another inmates), as *street women* (by the mistrust and contempt of the general public), and as *deviants* (by psychologists, criminologist, sociologists, and society). In the face of these overwhelmingly hostile forces, they can either accept their vulnerability and its consequences or believe they can control them through their own manipulations. My informants all appear to have, in various degrees, made the second choice. Their verbal manipulative skills are developed with care by practice, as a defensive and aggressive weapon—since both defence and aggression are intrinsically merged in survival. The informants' belief that they can, more or less, control their environment through manipulations does not necessarily conflict with the evidence of their frequent failure to do so. What it appears to do, is enable them to transform what might otherwise have to be seen as a *permanent, dispositional inability to cope* with their environment and their place in it, into a *temporary and situational failure of competence.*

In a "hustling" environment, where tradings of one sort or another, where communication and exchange are the lifeblood of the society on terms clearly defined by that society, classification of people and events is of primordial importance, since certain types of transactions are desirable between certain types of people, possible between certain types of people, possible only between certain types of people, or impossible between certain types of people.

Since the basis for a street woman's verbal manipulations is an understanding of her socio-economic environment and the place she occupies in it, she must first arrive at a definition of herself. The primary distinction she makes is between *straight* and *street,* and a secondary one between *male* and *female,* and in that environment of opposites, she must define herself as belonging to the street and being female.

THE STRAIGHT-STREET OPPOSITION

Other groups than street people have defined themselves in opposition to straight people: Hippies, gays, and cons (or ex-cons) for instance are members of subcultures which identify themselves in direct opposition to the straight culture. In a local newspaper report, a woman recently identified herself as straight, objecting to having been mistaken for a prostitute and been solicited. The opposition here appeared to be meant at the occupational level, and may or may not have included considerations on the related lifestyles and worldview. However, it is obvious that the basic oppositions *loose-straight, gay-straight, con-straight* entail much more than the sexual and legal differences on which they focus.

The opposition street-straight is an all-encompassing one. Straight, as the primary antithesis, stands for what society would define as *normal* in this limited context: reasonably monogamous, heterosexual, law abiding. What makes this paragon of societal virtues the arch-antagonist it is in these pairs of oppositions, is that it is the dominant and socially powerful member of the opposition. (It actually requires little effort of imagination to construct subsequent oppositions of terms such as poor-straight, female-straight, Indian-straight, etc. and still keep the basic straight characteristic attributes, while making the opposition a valid one).

The weakening of one constitutive element of the straight composite (as long as this element can itself be construed as straight in opposition to something else, e.g. gay or con) immediately cancels the whole. Thus the vulnerability of straightness as a whole makes it all the more determined to control or overpower its many sub-classificatory opposites. By the same token, it is equally essential for their survival that street people resist these attempts at controlling them. The constant comparison between what straight people do and say, and what street people do and say, serves to strengthen the latter's working stereotypes of the negative straight *(them)* and the positive street *(us)* with and within which to operate. It confirms the boundaries between the two groups and makes affiliations clear.

THE MALE-FEMALE OPPOSITION

The male-female dichotomy already mentioned as a secondary set of opposites often serves to strengthen the primary opposition since *straight men* and *street women* are the most frequently named trans-actors. But men are members of both cultures and in their dual straight and street aspects, they confuse the clear-cut delineation of the male-female and straight-street universes.

The street women studied here describe their relationship with street men as mutually supportive and their relationship with straight men as mutually exploitative. They further denounces the straight woman-straight man relationship as being also an exploitative one. In her own world, she recognizes many such relationships as well: prostitute-pimp, unfaithful old man-old lady. The only relationship they describe as non-exploitative is an idealized one between an old man who "looks after" his old lady (is faithful to her, appreciates her devotion to her work, protects her—usually afterwards in the form of retaliatory measures—against rip offs and bad tricks) and an old lady who "looks after" her old man (is faithful, is a good provider, does not complain about her work). This is identical to the one so often provided by a pimp's old lady (Milner & Milner 1972, Hall 1972) with, for the latter, the added satisfaction and prestige of seeing her pimp's elegance, style, and nonchalant enjoyment of his leisure, properly admired and envied. His style is her reward, since she provides for him by working around the clock, outside in all kinds of weather, facing humiliation and danger in all her encounters. All my informants, however, see these men as "leeches."

Since in both cases (old man and pimp) the woman's stand is identical, it is the sincerity of feelings of the man which provides for my informants the decisive distinction between a supportive and an exploitative relationship: The old man does not need to "sell" his "philosophy" (a term used by Jo to refer to the manipulative power of conviction of a pimp over his women) since he is deemed to be honest and sincere. From the man's sincerity stem other qualities which fill the woman's needs: faithfulness and appreciation. If sex, its performance and its avoidance, is the basis of a prostitute's transactions with tricks and marks, her personal relationships on the other hand are often full of sentimentality.[18] Her tattoos, for instance, often reflect her feelings. Bugsy drew for me the most popular tattoos in jail and on the street, as well as the one she was designing for herself as soon as she "could find

---

[18] I could not help thinking how appropriate was the location of the city's largest store of Harlequin Romances, on Granville Street, where most other stores on that particular stretch patronized by street walkers sold "adult" books or movies, or restricted "novelties."

somebody that can draw clasping hands." Her latest tattoo involved the transformation of her old man's initials into Dee's,[19] which could fortunately be done by the simple addition of a stroke, on the last initial, the first one being the same. Popular tattoos include the cowled figure of Death, or a tombstone bearing the two names, or more simply the lover's initials followed by T.D.D.U.P. (Till Death Do Us Part).

Significantly, it is often in her relationship with her female lovers that the street woman's need for affection, understanding, and companionship often appears best fulfilled. In the case of my informants, this may be partly explained by the fact that most of those sentimentally or sexually involved with other women were, when I talked to them, deprived of other romantic associations. Yet, my first impression that lesbian relationships were more supportive than the heterosexual ones—in the street life context—resulted from conversations on the street in 1975, where the heterosexual alternative existed. Many writers on prostitution mention the large and presumably above average proportion of lesbians among prostitutes. For instance, Limoges (1967:96) mentions that nine out of her twenty informants were lesbians. Through extended periods in jail, frequent interruptions of her relationship with a steady old man (because of his or her incarceration, for instance), increasing dissatisfaction with men as a whole whom she sees in their exploiters' role, a woman is sometimes led to substitute her ordinary male companion for a permanent or temporary female one in whom she finds the faithfulness, appreciation, and even the physical protection she seeks.

The description (in both the straight and street worlds) of the ideal and romantic relationship between two people is in fact asexual and stresses a mutually supportive sharing of values and defence against outsiders. Then, it is not surprising that this relationship should be best

---

[19] Limoges mentions that among Montreal prostitutes, the oldest tattoos display men's names and the most recent ones women's names (1967:95).

exemplified when joining together *street women* in a unified front against *men* and *straight people,* rather than in a more limited fashion against *straight men,* as in the more frequent heterosexual street associations.

Only when she substitutes an "old lady" for her "old man" does a street woman take her place in the simplified universe where *female-street-support* is directly opposed to *male-straight-exploitation* and does she acknowledge experiencing the exploitation of her body, mind, and earnings by all men, straight and street alike.

SUMMARY

To cope with the legal vulnerability and the social disvaluation of their position, female street addicts and prostitutes must acquire a competence which enables them to participate fully in the life of their subculture, where they find acceptance, understanding and support. As members of a subculture, they operate within the framework of the larger culture and appear to be constantly faced with their double and opposite values. Only by strictly defining this contradiction can the informants hope to define their own position and regulate their behaviour.

The manifestations of the essential incompatibility between the straight and street cultures form the core of the data. The sharp opposition between the two sets of cultural values is constantly brought into light. Since members of the subculture are cognizant of the value system of the larger culture, they use it to define their own by opposition. To explain a lifestyle in many ways opposite to the "normal" lifestyle (illegality of enterprise, nocturnal activity, venal and impersonal sex, immediate squandering of earnings, etc.) they describe a system of values opposite to the one of the larger society. Yet, the opposition lies not with the *professed* values of the larger society (generosity, prudence, enlightenment) but with what they see as being the *real* values of that society (greed, pusillanimity, ignorance).

These very values cause members of the larger and dominant society to try and take advantage of members of the subculture, female members in particular, and the latter feel justified in retaliating. Their own attempt at, and frequent success in, exploiting the other group, or defending themselves from its exploitation, take the form of verbal manipulations which they believe to have taken to a high level of expertise.

The goal of verbal manipulation is to make people behave in a manner that the manipulators see as profitable tothemselves. They can only do this through their knowledge of these people. From repeated encounters in specific circumstances with specific individuals, the informants elaborate broad and refined categories and constructs an interrelated system of values and relationships. The feedback elicited from each transaction serves to refine the classification, as the classification itself serves to regulate the transaction. As the informants' verbal manipulations are examined, they can only be understood in the context of the informatns' apprehension of their socio-economic environment and their subculture's system of values.

BIBLIOGRAPHY

Abrahams, Roger. 1968. "Introductory Remarks to a Rhetorical Theory of Folklore," *Journal of American Folklore* 81:141-158.

_____ 1970. "A Performance Centered Approach to Gossip," *Man* 5: 290-301.

_____ 1971. "Personal Power and Social Restraint in the Definition of Folklore," *Journal of American Folklore* 331:16-30.

_____ 1974. "Black Talking on the Street," in *Exploration in the Ethnography of Speaking*. Richard Baumand and Joel Sherzer, eds. Cambridge University Press.

Abrams, David and Brian Sutton-Smith. 1977. "The Development of the Trickster in Children's Narrative," *Journal of American Folklore* 355:29-47.

Agar, Michael. 1973. *Ripping and Running. A Formal Ethnography of Urban Heroin Addicts*. New York: Seminar Press.

_____ 1974. *Ethnography and Cognition*. Minneapolis: Burgess Publishing Company.

Albert, Ethel M. 1964. "Rhetoric," "Logic," and "Poetics" in Burundi: Culture Patterning of Speech Behavior," *American Anthropologist* 66(6) part 2: 35-54.

Anonymous. 1960. *Streetwalker.* New York: Viking Press.

Ardener, Shirley. 1975. "Sexual Insult and Female Militancy," in *Perceiving Women.* S. Arderner ed. London: Malaby Press.

Bahr, Howard, M. 1973. *Skid Road. An Introduction to Disaffiliation.* Oxford University Press.

Barth, Frederik. 1966. Models of Social Organization. Occasional paper No 23. Royal Anthropological Institute. London.

_____ 1966. "Introduction," in *Ethnic Groups and Boundaries. The Social Organization of Culture Difference,* Barth ed. Bergen-Oslo: Universitets Forlagets.

Bauman, Richard. 1971. "Differential Identity and the Social Base of Folklore." *Journal of American Folklore* 331:31-41.

Becker, Ernest. 1962. *The Birth and Death of Meaning.* New York: The Free Press.

Becker, Howard. 1963. *Outsiders: Studies in the Sociology of Deviance.* New York: The Free Press.

_____ 1968. "On Labeling Outsiders," in *Deviance. The Interactional Perspective.* E. Rubington and M.S. Weinberg, eds. New York: The MacMillan Company.

_____ 1970. Practitioner of Vice and Crime," in *Pathways to Data.* Robert Habenstein, ed. Chicago: Aldine.

Ben-Amos, Dan. 1971. "Toward a Definition of Folklore in Context," *Journal of American Folklore* 331:3-15.

Benjamin, Harry and R.E.L. Masters. 1964. *Prostitution and Morality.* A Definite Report on the Prostitute in Contemporary Society and an Analysis of the Causes and Effects of the Suppression of Prostitution. New York: Julian Press.

Berger, Peter L. and T. Luckmann. 1966. *The Social Construction of Reality: A Treatise in the Sociology of Knowledge.* New York: Doubleday.

Bernstein, Basil. 1964. "Elaborated and Restricted Codes: Their Social Origins and Some Consequences," *American Anthropologist* 66(6), part 2:55-69.

_____ 1973. "The Limits of my Language are Social," in *Rules and Meanings. The Anthropology of Everyday Knowledge.* Mary Douglas, ed. Hammonsworth: Penguin Books.

Berreman, Gerald. D. 1962. *Behind Many Masks.* Monograph No 4. Ithaca. New York Society for Applied Anthropology.

_____ 1972. "Is Ethnoscience Relevant?" in *Culture and Cognition: Rules, Maps and Plans*. James P. Spradley, ed. San Francisco: Chandler Publishing Company.

Black, Mary B. 1974. "Belief Systems," *in Handbook of Social and Cultural Anthropology*. John J. Honigmann, ed. Rand McNally College Publishing Company.

Black, Mary and Duane Metzger. 1965. Ethnographic Description and the Study of Law," *American Anthropologist* 67, part 2:141-165.

Blum, Richard. 1972. *Deceivers and Deceived*. Springfield, Ill: Charles C. Thomas.

Blumer, Herbert. 1972. "Symbolic Interaction," in *Culture and Cognition: Rules, Maps and Plans*. James P. Spradley, ed. San Francisco: Chandler Publishing Company.

Bovin, Mette. 1970. "Ethnic Stereotypes, Meaning and Use. A Comparative Study Based on the Literature and Field Material from Easter Niger." Unpublished manuscript.

Brown, L.B. 1973. *Ideology*. Penguin Books.

Bryan, James H. 1965. "Apprenticeship in Prostitution," *Social Problems* 13:278-297.

Burling, Robbins. 1969. "Linguistic and Ethnographic Description," *American Anthropologist* 71:817-827.

_____ 1970. *Man's Many Voices: Language in its Cultural Context*. New York: Holt, Rinehart and Winston, Inc.

Choisy, Maryse. 1965. *Psychoanalysis of the Prostitute.* New York: Pyramid Books.

Cohen, Albert, K. 1965. "The Sociology of the Deviant Act: Anomie Theory and Beyond," *American Sociological Review* 30:5-14.

Conklin, Harold C. 1969. "Comment," in *Cognitive Anthropology.* Tyler S. ed. New York: Holt, Rinehart and Winston, Inc.

Cothran, Kay, L. "Talking Trash in the Okefenoke Swamp Rim, Georgia," *Journal of American Folklore* 346:340-356.

Coutts, Dorothy Mae. 1961. "An Examination of the Social Structure of the Women's Unit, Oakalla Prison Farm." Unpublished M.A. Thesis. University of British Columbia.

Dallayrac, Dominique. 1966. *Dossier Prostitution.* Paris: Editions Robert Laffont.

Davis Johnson, Robbie. 1973. "Folklore and Women: A Social Interactional Analysis of the Folklore of a Texas Madam," *Journal of American Folklore* 341:211-224.

Dorson, Richard M. 1972. "Introduction: Concepts of Folklore and Folklife Studies," in *Folklore and Folklife. An Introductio.*, R.M. Dorson, ed. Chicago: The University of Chicago Press.

Douglas, Dorothy J. 1972. "Managing Fronts in Observing Deviance," in *Research on Deviance.* Jack Douglas ed. New York: Random House.

Douglas, Jack. 1970. "Deviance and Respectability: The Social Construction of Moral Meaning," in Deviance and Respectability. *The Social Construction of Moral Meanings.* J. Douglas, ed. New York: Basic Books, Inc.

Douglas, Mary, ed. 1972. *Rules and Meanings: The Anthropology of Everyday Knowledge.* Hammondsworth: Penguin Books.

Dundes, Alan, 1971. "Folk Ideas as Units of Worldview," *Journal of American Folklore* 331:93-103.

Erickson, Kai T. 1964. "Notes on the Sociology of Deviance," in *The Other Side. Perspectives on Deviance.* Howard S. Becker, ed. London: The Free Press of Glencoe.

Ervin-Tripp, Susan. 1964. "An Analysis of the Interaction of Language, Topic, and Listener," *American Anthropologist* 66(6), part 2:86-102.

Foster, George M. 1967. "Peasant Society and the Image of Limited Good," in *Peasant Society. A Reader.* Jack M. Potter, May N. Diaz, George M. Foster, eds. Boston: Little, Brown and Co.

Frake, Charles O. 1964. "How to ask for a Drink in Subanun," *American Anthropologist* 66(6), part 2:127-132.

_____ 1969. "The Ethnographic Study of Cognitive Systems," in *Cognitive Anthropology*. S. Tyler, ed. New York: Holt, Rinehart and Winston.

Gallantin Anderson, Barbara. 1974. "The Changing French Woman: Her Challenged World," in *Many Sisters. Women in Cross-Cultural Perspectives*. C. J. Matthiasson, ed. New York: The Free Press.

Geerts, Clifford. 1973. *The Interpretation of Cultures*. New York: Basic Books.

Goffman, Erving. 1952. "On Cooling the Mark Out: Some Aspects of Adaptation to Failure," *Psychiatry. Journal for the Study of Interpersonal Processes* 15:451-463.

_____ 1959. *Presentation of Self in Everyday Life*. Garden City, N.Y.: Doubleday Anchor Books.

_____ 1963a. *Behavior in Public Places*. New York: The Free Press.

_____ 1963b. *Stigma: Notes on the Management of Spoiled Identity*. Englewood Cliffs, N.J.: Prentice Hall.

_____ 1964 "The Neglected Situation," *American Anthropologist* 66(6). Part 2:133-136.

_____ 1969. *Strategic Interaction. An Analysis of Doubt and Calculation in Face-to-Face, Day-to-Day Dealings with One Another*. New York: Ballantine Books.

Goodenough, Ward. H. 1957. "Cultural Anthropology and Linguistics," in Report of the Seventh Annual Round Table Meeting on Linguistic and Language Study. P.L. Garvin, ed. Georgetown University Monograph Series on Language and Linguistics, No 9, Washington.

_____ 1969. "Rethinking 'Status' and 'Role.' Toward a General Model of Cultural Organization of Social Relationships, " in *Cognitive Anthropology*. S. Tyler, ed. New York: Holt, Rinehart and Winston.

_____ 1971. *Culture, Language and Society*. Addison-Wesley Publishing Company, Inc.

Graven, Jean. 1962. *L'Argot et le tatouage des criminels. Etude de criminology sociale*. Neuchâtel: Editions de la Bacconière.

Greenwald, Harold. 1970. *The Elegant Prostitute. A Social and Psychoanalytical Study*. New York: Walker and Company.

Gumperz, John J. 1964. "Linguistic and Social Interaction in Two Communities," *American Anthropologist* 66(6), part 2:137-163.

Hall, Edward T. 1964. "Adumbration as a Feature of the Intellecutal Communication," In *American Anthropologist* 66(6), part 2:154-163.

Hall Susan. 1972. *Gentlemen of Leisure*. New York: The New American Library.

_____ 1973. *Ladies of the Night*. New York: Simon & Schuster, Inc.

Halliday, M.A.K. 1976. "Anti-Languages," *American Anthropologist* 76:570-584.

Harris, Marvin. 1968. *The Rise of Anthropological Theory*. New York: Thomas Y. Cromwell Company.

Hays, Terence E. 1968. "A Bat by Any Other Name is a Bird: Folk Taxonomy and Cognitive Studies," *Colorado Anthropologist* 1:1-17.

Henslin, James M. 1968. "Trust and the Cab Driver," in *Sociology and Everyday Life*. M. Truzzi, ed. Englewood Cliffs, N.J.: Prentice Hall, Inc.

Hirschi, Travis. 1962. "The Professional Prostitute," *Berkeley Journal of Sociology* 7:33-49.

Humphreys, Laud. 1970. *The Tearoom Trade: Impersonal Sex in Public Places*. Chicago: Aldine.

Hymes, Dell H. 1962. "The Ethnography of Speaking," in *Anthropology and Behavior*. Thomas Gladwin and W.C. Sturtevant, eds. Anthropological Society of Washington

_____ 1964. "Introduction: Toward Ethnographies of Communication," *American Anthropologist* 66(6), Part 2:1-34.

_____ 1971. "The Contribution of Folklore to Sociolinguistic Research," *Journal of American Folklore* 331:93-103.

Irwin, John and Donald R. Cressey. 1064. "Thieves, Convicts and the Inmate Culture," in *The Other Side. Perspectives on Deviance*. Howard S. Becker, ed. London: The Free Press of Glencoe.

Jackman, Norman, Richard O'Toole, Gilbert Geis. 1963. "The Self-Image of the Prostitute," *The Sociological Quaterly* 4:150-160. Also in *Deviance. The Interactionist Perspective,* Rubington and Weinbers, eds. New York: The MacMillan Company, 1968.

Jackson, Bruce. 1974. *In the Life. Versions of the Criminal Experience*. New York: Mentor Books.

James, Jennifer. 1971. "A Formal Analysis of Prostitution in Seattle," Final Report I, "Basic Statistical Summary.

_____ 1972a. Ethnographic Semantic Approaches to the Study of an Urban Subculture: Streetwalkers." Unpublished Ph.D dissertation. University of Washington.

_____ 1972b. "Two Domains of Streetwalker Argot," *Anthropological Linguistics* 14:172-181.

_____ 1972c. "Sweet Cream Ladies: An Introduction to the Prostitute Taxonomy," *Canadian Journal of Anthropology* 3:102-118.

_____ 1977. "Ethnography and Social Problems," *in Street Ethnography: Selected Studies of Crime and Drug Use in Natural*

Settings. Robert S, Weppner, ed. Beverley Hills: Sage Publications.

Jones, Edward E. and Richard E. Nesbett. 1971. *The Actor and the Observer: Divergent Perceptions of the Causes of Behavior.* New York: General Learning Press: University Press.

Jung, C.G. 1956. "Commentary," in *The Trickster: A Study in American Indian Mythology.* P. Radin ed. New York: Philosophical Press.

Kantrowitz, Nathan. 1967. "The Vocabulary of Race Relations in a Prison." Paper presented before the American Dialect Society at the annual meeting of the Modern Language Association, Chicago.

_____ 1968. "A Vocabulary of 'Inmate Culture' in a Prison," paper presented at the annual meeting of the American Sociological Association, Boston.

Kaplan, Howard B. 1975. *Self-Attitudes and Deviant Behaviour.* Pacific Palisades, Cal: Goodyear Publishing Company, Inc.

Kerhaghan, Patrick. 1075. "An Unqualified Look at Rounders. Non-Statistical Understanding of the Clients," unpublished manuscript. Vancouver, B.C.

Kitsuse, John I. 1968. Societal Reaction to Deviant Behavior," in *Deviance. The Interactionist Perspective.* E. Rubington and M.S. Wienberg, eds. New York: The MacMillan Company.

_____ 1972. "Deviance, Deviant Behavior, Deviance: Some Conceptual Problems," in *The Production of Deviance*. W. Filstead, ed. New York: Markham Press.

Klockars, Carl. 1974. *The Professional Fence*. New York: The Free Press.

Kochman, Thomas. 1970. "'Rapping' in the Black Ghetto," *TransAction* 6:24-34.

Köngäs Maranda. E.K. and Pierre Maranda. 1970. *Structural Models in Folklore and Transformational Essays*. The Hague: Mouton.

Layton, Monique. 1975. "Prostitution in Vancouver (1973-1975): Official and Unofficial Reports." Report to the British Columbia Police Commission. Victoria: Department of the Attorney-General.

_____ 1979. "The Ambiguities of the Law or the Streetwalker's Dilemma," *Chitty's Law Journal* 27:109-120.

Leach, Edmund. 1964. "Anthropological Aspects of Language: Animal Categories and Verbal Abuse," In *New Directions in the Study of Language*. Eric H. Lenneberg, ed. Massachussetts Institute of Technology Press.

Letkemann, Peter J. 1971. "Modus Operandi: Crime as Work," Ph.D. dissertation. University of British Columbia.

_____ 1973. *Crime as Work*. Englewood Cliffs, N.J.: Prentice-Hall.

Liebow, Elliot. 1966. *Tally's Corner. A Study of Negro Streetcorner Men.* Boston: Little, Brown and Company.

Limoges, Thérèse. 1967. *La prostitution à Montréal.* Montréal: Les éditions de l'homme.

Lofland, Lyn H. 1969. "Self-Management in Public Settings," *Urban Life and Culture* 1:93-108.

Lyman, Stanford M. and Marvin B. Scott. 1968. "Coolness in Everyday Life," in *Sociology and Everyday Life.* Mr. Truzzi, ed. Englewood Cliffs, N.J.: Prentice-Hall, Inc.

McCaghy, Charles H. and James K. Skipper. 1969, "Lesbian Behavior as an Adaptation to the Occupation of Stripping," *Social Problems* 17(2).

McCall, George J. and J.L. Simmons. 1966. *Identities and Interactions.* New York: The Free Press.

McIntosh, Mary. 1971. "Changes in the Organization of Thieving," in *Images of Deviance.* Stanley Cohen, ed. Penguin Books.

Matza, David W. 1969. *Becoming Deviant.* Englewood Cliffs, N.J.: Prentice-Hall, Inc.

Maurer, David W. 1939. "Prostitutes and Criminal Argot," *The American Journal of Sociology* 44:546-550.

_____ 1940. *The Big Con. The Story of the Confidence Man and the Confidence Game*. New York: Pocket Books, Inc.

Mauss, Marcel. 1969. *The Gift. Forms and Functiones of Exchange in Archaic Societies*. London: Cohen & West Limited.

Merton, R.K. 1963. "Social Structure and Anomie," in *Social Theory and Social Structure*. New York.

Millett, Kate. 1971. *The Prostitution Papers. A Candid Dialogue*. New York: Basic Books, Inc.

Mills, James. 1972. *Report to the Commissioner*. New York: Farrar, Strauss and Giroux.

Milner, Christina and Richard Milner. 1972a. *Black Players. The Secret World of Black Pimps*. New York: Bantam.

Milner, Richard. 1972b. "Trickster, Bad Nigga, and Urban Ethnography," *Urban Life and Culture* 1:109-117.

Newton, Esther. 1972. *Mother Camp: Female Impersonators in America*. Englewood Cliffs, N.J.: Prentice-Hall, Inc.

Olesen, Virginia L. and Elvi Whittaker. 1966. "Adjudication of Student Awareness in Professional Socialization: The Language of Laughter and Silences," *The Sociological Quaterly* 7:381-396.

_____ 1967. "Role-Making in Participant Observation: Processes in the Researcher-Actor Relationship," *Human Organization* 26:273-281.

_____ 1968. *The Silent Dialogue. A Study in the Social Psychology of Professional Socialization*. San Francisco: Jossey Bass, Inc.

Pike, Kenneth, L. 1966. "Etic and Emic Standpoints for the Description of Behavior," in *Language in Relation to a Unified Theory of the Structure of Human Behavior*. The Hague: Mouton.

Pilcher, William W. 1972. *The Portland Longshoremen. A Dispersed Urban Community*. New York: Holt, Rinehart and Winston.

Polsky, Ned. 1969. *Hustlers, Beats and Others*. Garden City, N.Y.: Anchor Books.

Preble, Edward and John J. Casey. 1969. "Taking Care of Business. The Heroin User's Life on the Street," *The International Journal of Addictions* 4:1-24.

Psathas, George. 1972. "Ethnoscience and Ethnomethodology," in *Culture and Cognition: Rules, Maps and Plans*. James P. Spradley, ed. San Francisco: Chandler Publishing Company.

Radcliffe-Brown, A.R. 1952. *Structure and Function in Primitive Society*. London: Cohen & West Limited.

Radin, Paul. 1956. *The Trickster: A Study in American Indian Mythology*. New York: Philosophical Library.

Reiss, Jr. Albert. 1968. "The Social Interation of Queers and Peers," in *Deviance. The Interactionist Perspective*. E. Rubington and M.S. Weinbert, eds. New York: The MacMillan Co.

Rolph, C.H., ed. 1955. *Women of the Street*. London: Secker & Warburg.

Rosnow, Ralph L. and Gary Alan Fine. 1976. *Rumor and Gossip. The Social Psychology of Hearsay*. New York: Elsevier Scientific Publishing Company.

Rumack, Martin. 1972. "Prostitution: A Penal or a Medical Problem," *Chitty's Law Journal*.

Sartre, Jean-Paul. 1963. Saint-Genêt: Actor and Martyr. New York: George Brazilier.

Scott, Marvin and Stanford Lyman. 1968. "Accounts," *American Sociological Review* 23:46-62.

_____ 1970. "Accounts, Deviance and Social Order," in *Deviance and Respectability: The Social Construction of Moral Meanings*. Jack D. Douglas, ed. New York: Basic Books.

Schutz, Alfred. 1967. *The Phenomenology of the Social World*. Northwestern University Press.

Searle, John R. 1969. *Speech Acts. An Essay in the Philosophy of Language*. Cambridge University Press.

Sheehy, Gail. 1974. *Hustling*. New York: Dell Publishing Co.

Simmons, J. L. 1965. "Public Stereotypes of Deviants," *Social Problems* 13:223-232.

Skipper. J. K. and C. H. Macghy. 1970. "Strip-Teasers: The Anatomy and Career Contingencies of a Deviant Occupation." *Social Problems* 17:391-405.

Slim, Iceberg. 1969a. *Trick Baby. The Biography of a Con Man.* Los Angeles: Holloway Publishing Co.

_____ 1969b. Pimp. *The Story of My Life.* Los Angeles: Holloway Publishing Co.

Spradley, James P. 1970. *You Owe Yourself a Drunk: An Ethnography of Urban Nomads.* Boston: Little, Brown and Company.

_____ 1972a. "Foundations of Cultural Knowledge," in *Culture and Cognition: Rules, Maps and Plans.* James P. Spradley, ed. San Francisco: Chandler Publishing Company.

_____ 1972b. "Adaptive Strategies of Urban Nomads," in *Culture and Cognitio:; Rules, Maps and Plans. James* P. Spradley, ed. San Francisco: Chandler Publishing Company.

_____ 1972c. "Bending the Drunk Charge," in *Culture and Cognition: Rules, Maps and Plans.* James P. Spradley, ed. San Francisco: Chandler Publishing Company.

Spradley, James P. and Brenda Mann. 1975. *The Cocktail Waitress. Woman's Work in a Man's World.* New York: John Wiley & Sons.

Stack, Carol. 1974. *All Our Kin. Strategies for Survival in a Black Community*. New York: Harper & Row.

Stewart, George Lee. 1972. "On First Being a John," *Urban Life and Culture* 1:255-274.

Stoddart, Kenneth. 1968. "Drug Transactions; The Social Organization of a Deviant ctivity,' unpublished M.A. thesis. University of British Columbia.

Sturtevant, W. C. 1964. "Studies in Ethnoscience," *American Anthropologist* 66(6), part 2.

Sutherland, Edwin. 1937. *The Professional Thief.* Chicago: University of Chicago Press.

Sutter, Alan G. 1066. "The World of the Righteous Dope Fiend," *Issues in Criminology* 2:177-222.

Sykes, Gresham M. and David Matza. 1968. "On Neutralizing Deliquent Self-Image," in *Deviance, The Interactionist Perspective*. E. Rubington and Ms. Weinberg, eds. New York: The KacMillan Company.

Tyler, Stephen. 1969. "Introduction," in *Cognitive Anthropology*. S. Tyler, ed. New York: Holt, Rinehart and Winston.

Tochs, Hans. 1969. *Violent Men*. Chicago: Aldine.

Truzzi, Marcello, ed. 1968. *The Sociology of Everyday Life*. Englewood Cliffs, N.J.: Prentice-Hall, Inc.

Velarde, Albert. 1975. "Become Prostituted. The Decline of the Massage Parlour Profession and the Masseuse," *The British Journal of Criminology* 15:251-263.

Weppner, Robert S. 1973. "An Anthropological View of the Street Addict's World," *Human Organization* 32:111-121.

Werner, Oscar. 1973. "Cultural Knowledge, Language and World View," in *Cognition: A Multiple View*. Paul Gavin, ed. New York: Spartan Books.

Whittaker, Elvi. 1973. "Explanations and Realities: The World of the Mainland Migrant to Hawaii." Paper read at the annual meeting of the C.S.A.A., Kingston, Ontario.

Whyte, William Foote. 1943. *Street Corner Society*. Chicago: Chicago University Press.

_____ 1948. *Human Relations in the Restaurant Industry*. New York: McGraw-Hill Book Company.

Wilson, James Q. 1975. *Thinking About Crime*. New York: Basic Books, Inc.

Winn, Denise. 1974. *Prostitutes*. London: Hutchinson.

Young, Jock. 1971. *The Drugtakers. The Social Meaning of Drug Use*. London: Granada Publishing Ltd.

Zucker, Hall. 1955. *Tattoed Women and Their Mates.* World Folk Art Series, No1, Philadelphia: Andre Levy.

APPENDIX A

BASIC GLOSSARY

Cops, also known as *pigs* and *bulls,* are police officers. *Harness bulls* are officers in uniform (although some people reserve the term for policemen on horseback or motorcycle policemen). *Narcs* are the much hated members of the Narcotic Squad, and *undercover* is used to describe members of the same squad who infiltrate the drug subculture. *Asshole* (although the term is not exclusively reserved for them) is often used to describe an *ignorant* cop who abuses his powers.

Dope is a general term for drug, although among *junkies* it refers mostly to heroin. Drug is basically divided into *downers (bombers,* barbiturates, heroin) and *uppers* (amphetamines, *speed, coke, acid,* MDA, etc. and *smoke dope: hash* and *pot).* They can also be mixed (e.g. *speed balls).* *Junk* and *stuff* are the most frequently used terms for heroin. Other terms, less commonly used in Vancouver, are: *heroin* (only used when talking to a non-user straight person), *skag, shmeck* (an old term still used by "old dope fiends") which became *smack* in the 1960s, and *shit. Horse, H, snow* (also referring to cocaine) and *jazz* are known here but said to be mostly used in the United States.

The terms *user* and *junkie* (i.e. user of *junk)* are comparatively recent. Stoddart's informants (1968) always refer to "fiends" or "dope fiends," a term which is found in all the older texts. The terms *trafficker, connection,* and *man,* are used at many levels of the business of selling illegal drugs. On the street, people *put out* caps (gelatin capsules in which units of heroin are sold in Canada) or *bundles* (25 caps) for a *dealer* or *middle man* who handles bundles or ounces (400 caps). Pure heroin is cut down with milk sugar and his being sold in weak concentration in Vancouver.

Heroin can be absorbed by *sniffing, skin popping* (subcutaneous injections) or *mainlining* (intravenous injections). A *rig* or *outfit* (syringe, needle, and bottle cap) is used to mix and inject it. Collapsed veins and hepatitis are frequently the result of mainlining. A *blast* or *rush* immediately follows the administration of heroin, itself later followed by a *nodding* period of contentment. A *wired* (addicted) person will feel *sick* when he cannot *score* (buy) and *fix.* These withdrawal pains make it all the more difficult to quit or *kick* the *habit.*

Hooker is, with *working girl,* the most general and most generally acceptable term for "prostitute." For a description of various types of hookers (*chippie, weekend hooker, summertime hooker, call girl, massage parlour* and *steam bath hooker, camp to camp hooker, stag girl, street girl, sleazy, hooker on the boats, old-timer, turn out, rip off, out of town girl, main lady, hustler*) see the text.

A *mark* often started as a *trick,* but has developed a more permanent and more elaborate relationship with a woman and is reported to provide money, goods, and services in exchange for whatever she is willing to give him. Most women simply list him among the tricks. A mark is also a con artist's non-sexual victim.

A *trick* is a prostitute's customer. The once familiar term *John* does not seem to be used much any more, in this city at least, except as in *square Johns,* which applies to straight people in general. For a description of various types of *tricks (East Indian, pervert, freak, sadist, weirdo, drunk, greenhorn, student, fast trick, regular or steady trick, servicemen, Greek sailor, straight trick, old men, masochist, Oriental, talker),* see the text.

A *trick* also refers to the professional services rendered: to *turn a trick*, or can also refer to a certain type of trick turned (e.g. a *car trick*, a *double trick*).

APPENDIX B

TAXONOMY

APPENDIX B : TAXONOMY (DRUGS)

DRUG SCENE

METHODS of administration	DRUGS (DOPE) — UPPERS	DRUGS (DOPE) — DOWNERS	DRUGS (DOPE) — MIXED	USERS	TRAFFICKERS
smoking	SMOKE DOPE: hash	DOPE: junk	speed balls (heroin & cocaine)	user	dealer
popping	pot – grass	stuff		junkie	pusher
snorting	pep pills	shit		hype	middle man
blowing	speed	smack		to be wired	connection man
sniffing	meth	skag		head	
skin popping	crystal	(other terms are used in the States)		hophead	
shooting	coke	bombers		acid freak	
mainlining	acid	barbiturates (Tuinal)		pill freak	
cranking up	MDA	mescaline			
	angel dust	methadone			
		Valium			
		glue			

EFFECTS

- high
- rush – blast
- dozing
- nodding
- yen
- being sick

APPENDIX B : TAXONOMY (STREET / STRAIGHT)

MEANS OF LIVELIHOOD	STREET		STRAIGHT			
	STREET PEOPLE	MARGINAL PEOPLE	STRAIGHT INVOLVED WITH THE STREET	COPS	"AUTHORITIES"	UNINVOLVED SQUARE JOHNS ON THE STREET
welfare	rounders	teeny boppers	tricks	cops	lawyers	shoppers
living off a mark	street hookers	chippie hypes	marks	pigs	judges	movie goers
hooking	users	chippie hookers	fences	bulls	probation off.	waiting at the bus stop .
shoplifting	dealers	summertime h.	straight dealers	harness bulls	parole off.	
boosting		weekend hook.	guys at the desk (hotels)	plainclothes	counsellors	
rehashing				morality	social workers	
paper hanging			guys you have to piece off	narcs	matrons	
B & E			cabbies	undercover	guards	
trafficking				the Man		
putting out				rats		
ripping off drunks						

Appendix C: street maps

APPENDIX E

Robson Street

Smythe Street

Nelson Street

Helmcken Street

Davie Street

Drake Street

THE DOWNTOWN AREA

BP: Beer parlour
H: Hotel
B: Bar
C: Club, Cabaret

223

APPENDIX E

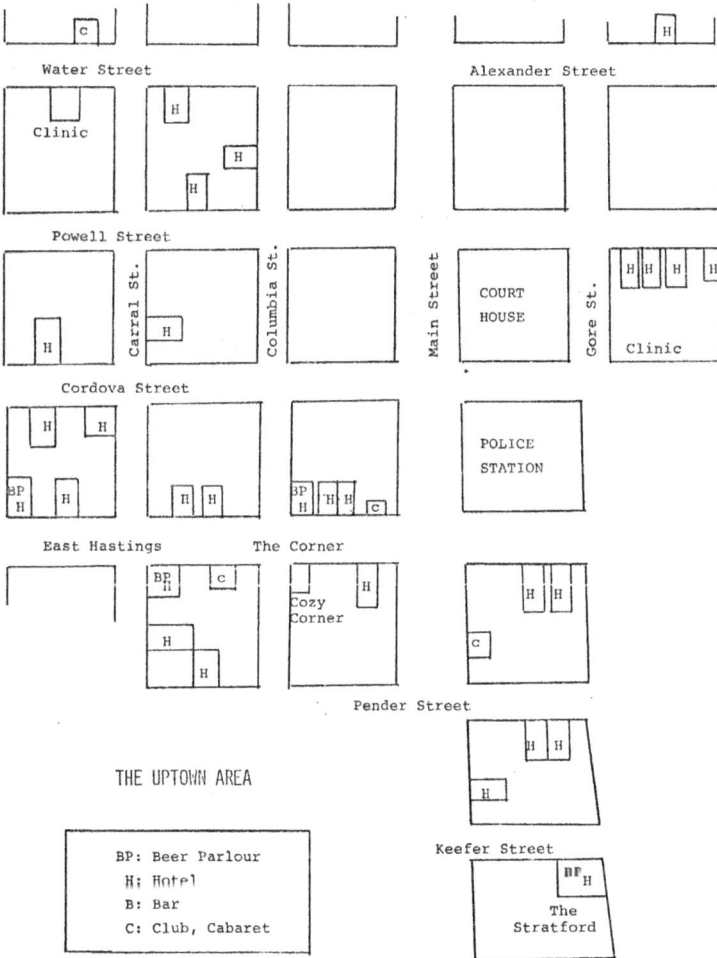

Water Street

Alexander Street

Clinic

Powell Street

Carral St.

Columbia St.

Main Street

COURT
HOUSE

Gore St.

H H H H

Clinic

Cordova Street

H

H

POLICE
STATION

BP
H

H

BP
H

H H

C

East Hastings   The Corner

BP
H

C

Cozy
Corner

H

H H

C

H

H

H

Pender Street

THE UPTOWN AREA

H H

H

BP: Beer Parlour
H: Hotel
B: Bar
C: Club, Cabaret

Keefer Street

BP
H

The
Stratford

APPENDIX D
A SAMPLE OF STORIES

The twelve stories below were not selected to offer a representative view of the concerns of the street or the significant events which are seen as occurring there. If this had been the case, a story about hassling by asshole pigs should have, for instance, balanced the restrain of Bugsy's cop stories. However, the selection attempts to be representative of the style of the stories collected. "The English Duke," pronounced "Dook" (#l), for instance, was not so much selected because of its content as because of its form: It is the shortest and best defined of the long, rambling tales which, in their original form, may make somewhat tedious reading, and which were mostly used for extracts illustrating specific points. On the other hand, "The Little Old Man" (#10) is a good example of the brief anecdote which, in an even shorter version, may be passed on for a good laugh.

#1 *THE ENGLISH DUKE* (by BOOTS)
I met this guy on Granville and he come up with this limousine and the two guys. He come up the stairs and he asked me if I wanted to go out and I said, "Well, who's with you?" And he said, "It's a goon squad." I asked, "What's the goon squad?" He said it was his bodyguards. Well ...What would you think if you saw a guy with a black limousine? I thought he was a bull, or something! He comes up the stairs and he asked me how much I want and I told him, "Fifty bucks and some." He comes in and I told him, "Take off your gear and get to bed." But, no. First he wanted me to get out. And I didn't know who he was. I thought he was just some guy, you know. But he wanted me to go to his hotel ... His body guards stood outside the door, so I went to the manager, you see, to make sure that these guys don't get me. I thought they were his friends, or something. Well, he reels in there and finishes our trick and goes out.

Next day, the guy comes with 200 dollars and the limousine and his bodyguards, and asked me to come for dinner. I said, "Where to?" He said, "The Villa Hotel." They had a whole floor booked up! The third floor. So, I wouldn't get in the car. So, he come back and he said, "There's 200 dollars just to come to the dining room with me, please." So, I went and had a steak and lobster and it was really good, and I left with the 200 dollars. So, all the time he was here, he came every day, every night. Twice a day, 400 bucks a day. And I'd go and eat breakfast with him and then dinner.

So, then he goes to leave. The day before he left, it come on the radio! His first name ... And I listen and listen, and it's his voice! I couldn't believe it ... He was a duke! I was so embarrassed! He come that night and he said, "Well, I will have to leave tomorrow morning, and I want to know if you'll spend the night." "Well, we have my hotel ..." "No," he said, "you come to my place, it will be all right." So I come to the Villa ... Got all the floors roped off and that. I walked … The elevator door opened and about four doors opened around his room ... So I stayed the night with him ... 500 dollars. Next morning, I went to leave. I told him I had to go downtown to score. He didn't know what "score" means! He's really *stupid!* He told me ... I was asking what he was doing with a hustler around, you know. So, his wife died last year, or something, and his son got killed the same day my old man got killed. So, he said, "I'd really like to take you back to England with me!" So, I said: "Well, I can't go, you know," I said. "I got lots of things to do," I said. "How am I gonna score over in England?" He said, "Don't worry about that," you know. So, I says, "I can't get across anyway, you know ... I got my charges and that, and they're not going to let me cross the border." He said, "With my name on your passport, they'll let you cross, they'll *have* to! There's no way anybody can stop you from moving around with me."

I went down to the Aristocratic Restaurant to score. I told him to meet me there before he left. He pulls up in his car, while I was waiting there. I says, "Well, you're going, hey?" He says, "Well, yeah ... Just get in the car with me!" I says, "Fuck you!" He says, "Come on, just get in and talk to me before I go." I went to get in the car and he told the guy to take off with me, you know. So, I says. "The hell with you! ... Fuck you! ..."

Now he writes to me all the time ... Four, five times a week. Invites me over there ... But if I go over to England, they'll turn me into a Duchess or something! I told him I like Granville Street. He says, "Do you think this is your whole life? Once I got you over to England," he says, "give you what your heart desire ... *Anything,*" he said, "that you *ever* dreamed ..." he said, "You wouldn't want to come back!" He said, "You might miss Vancouver at first," he said, "but once you're over there you'll be all right." Well, he's just going to take me over there and turn me into one of them! When I'm over there, I can't do anything ... See, here, I'm on my ground ... I just whistle and someone comes runnin'! But, over there, I don't know anybody.

He writes to me ... He's been here seven, eight times ... He phones long distance all the time. He'd talk to the manager of the hotel because I wouldn't get on the phone. I'd be standing right there, and he'd say, *"Please,* talk her into comin' I'll send the jet over for her!" So, the guy says, "Oh, that's right ... yeah ... yeah ... Be a good thing for her ..." And I'd just stand there, laughing. And he'd be crying over the phone! And this is a *Duke!* Stupid!!

I told him I'd take his money, but that would be about it. I said, "Go and marry one of your duchess!" But no ... He writes all the time ... He wanted to go to court for me ... Tell the Judge that he wanted to marry me, look after me, and plead not to put me in jail, and that he'd be responsible for my actions from then on ... Crazy idiot! He didn't even know what "junk" was! He hadn't even heard of it! When I told him I had to go fix. FIX ... He didn't even know what it was!

He just likes me because I'm different to what he's used to. He'd never even gone to the park by himself before. I took him to the park. His bodyguards thought he'd get lost and somebody would bump him off! Oh, they hated me! He used to tell me, you know. I said, "What do they think of me?" He said, "They just shake their head." I'd bang around up there and make noise and knock on the doors, and tell them I hoped they were getting off, listening to him all the time! I don't know how he could live like that! He had a guy to dress him! Bring him his clothes and lay them out for him ... Taking away his pyjamas. I used to tell him, "You're retarded! You can't even dress yourself?" But he said that's the way they were brought up.

I'd get knocked up or something, and then he'd have a kid to take over his ... whatchamacallit? ... because he never had any more kids after that one boy that was killed. But he's a nice guy ... I've got a letter from him just last week. He's coming over soon on business. He asked me to visit him. I said no. I wrote back and told him I was too busy, much too busy ... I told him to send me some money ... After all the money he gave me!

#2   *THE SPECIAL TRICK* (by BOOTS)

This guy comes into town, and he was known for spending thousands of dollars on a girl the first time she went out ...I just told my old man that I was going out with this guy. Well, he knew the guy's name right away when I said that! So, he just told me he knew the guy and what to do, and I went out and do it. I got $15,000 dollars for it. He still sends me money, but I'm no good anymore, because he's *used* me, right? But he still sends me a couple of hundred dollars at Christmas and stuff like that. My old man told me, "When you go out with him, don't get into bed with him." He said, "Kid him around as long as you can without giving him anything. That's what he likes." He says, "You've got to be smart. You've got to know when to give a little bit more ..."

I had every hustling broad in town rooting for me, trying to tell me what to do, because they'd all gone with him before! I got help from them. Because they knew *they* couldn't get hold of the money. It was sitting there, you know ... and they knew they'd get pieced off. So, they said, "He really likes this ..." Once he has you, that's it. He'll be nice, he'll take you to dinner, but there's nothing else ... Like, a coupla times he took me to dinner right after and he'd start asking me, "Can't you get me someone that's never gone out with a guy before?" you know. So I got him another girl and she went with him and got quite a bit of money off him and then she turn on somebody else to him. He likes that. All he does is work all year and then he comes into town for his holidays and he spends everything he's made that year in a coupla weeks. And then, that's it! He goes back out to work. He runs cats *[Caterpillar tractors]* or something like that ... We know what to gain and we know what to give and we both live by the rules, and we both can come out winners. But there's not many guys like that around.

#3 *THE MARK'S WIFE* (by BOOTS)

One of the guy's wives ... He was the second trick I ever gone out with. Her and I are now best friends! She come down and was gonna cut my throat! ... I didn't know who he was. I thought he was a nice-looking guy. I had just turned out and I thought he's a good trick ... He's nice ... He spent his money like it is gone out of style. And he was nice ... Ugh . . I stuck out much too long, because she come down with the hood down to Granville Street. I was coming out of the hotel with him, my arm through his . . Oh God! You never seen a broad so mad! She said she was gonna cut my throat from ear to ear ... I was young then ... Oh, she terrified me! And now, we're the best of friends. We've been best friends for a year and a half. At first she was really nasty to me. She'd got my phone number, and about a month after she tried to put a beating on me when she saw us in the hotel, she started phoning me. First, she was really nasty. Then she said: "What does he say about me when he's there?" "Oh, he says how much he loves you and that ..." I just told her a story. Then she got to be really nice, and she asked me one day to meet her, and she was really upset because he'd gone to see me, she said. "He's with some other broad!" She was all upset about this because he'd gone to see a hooker ... I said "Look at it ... It's for the money ... Do you think I'd go and chase him? Forget it! When his money's all gone, I don't want no more to do with him!" So, she grew accustomed to that. But when she found that he'd seen some other broad, then she flipped and she come to me!" Told me to get him back! So I went to get him back. Told him not to see that girl again. Now, she's one of my best friends.

#4   *THE TRICK'S WIFE* (by BUGSY)

Well, there was this guy I used to go out with quite often. And I knew he was married. And his wife come downtown one night, and she says, "Your name is Bugsy?" She says, "I want to talk to you." And I says, "Oh, yeah? Who are you?" She says, "Well, I'm Joe's wife." Eeeeeek ... Oh, oh ... I'm in for shit! But we went into the Blackstone Hotel and we settled down, having a few drinks. And she was talking to me. And she says, "Joe seems a lot happier when he comes home at night." And I says, "Oh, does he?" And I says, "Wait a minute! What's your gimmick?" I says, "What are you doing?" She says, "Nothing." She says, "I just wanted to thank you for helping Joe and I stay together, 'cause we were on the verge of a divorce." I says, "Well, I'm glad I helped out somebody." So Joe come in the bar just out there and I says, "Oh, brother! This is all I need!" Cause Joe used to walk in the bar all the time and put his arm around me. Well, he come in the bar, sat between us, and he put his arm around me and her. And they were going to Hawaii and they asked me if I wanted to go with them! And I says no, like a stupid fool! And then Joe and I were talking for a while, and I was gonna go. In fact, I was just gonna go when I ended up here! I'd be in Hawaii right now .

It was mainly a sex problem between them. "The same old thing all the time," that's what Joe said. He said he couldn't handle it, he said she refused to do it in a different way because she didn't know how. She was scared. She always had that Mommy image in her head: "Don't do that! That's a naughty girl!" Before they left, I had a long talk with her, and I told her, "Read that "Hundred and One Different Positions." It'll do you a lot of good." I says, "You could help yourself as well as Joe," and I says, "You could be happily married and he won't have to come down here looking for girls!"

#5   *HIDING JUNK* (by BUGSY)

I remember one time, I had a cap. I had just scored and the cops were walking up, and I had nowhere to put it. I had no bra on, and a halter top, a little skimpy halter top, not even ... This thing I got on now, I got more than I got on. So ... The cops were coming, so I took it and stuck it in my ear! But I didn't realize I pushed it down too far, and I tried everything to get this thing out, and it wouldn't come out! So I went to the hospital. I says, "I got something stuck in my ear." And the doctor says, "Yeah? Let me see!" and he looked and he says, "What is it?" And I says, "Oh, one of my pills, one of my medications," I says, "I take some medication," I says, "I take that for epilepsy," and he says, "That looks more like heroin to me." I says, "Hey, will you just get it outta there, it's killing me!" So he pulled it out and he says, "Yeah, it looks like heroin," and I says, "It ain't!" and I took off! I had one hell of a time getting the cap opened. Finally, I just took it and broke the end off it, because there was all the wax from the ear on it, and I poured it in, and I had one hell of a time fixin'.

#6   *A LOVE STORY* (by BUGSY)

There was this sailor ... He wasn't a Greek, though, he was an American. And I fell in love with him. I just found out that he died at sea. They made a potato brew, and it was all poisoned. I didn't believe the guy when he told me, because they've usually got tons of beer on board. He says, "Well, the beer was all knocked off and they were told they were not allowed to carry anymore beer." So they were making a potato brew. Him and two other guys died from it. But that's a different story. Him… Oh, that's one night I'll *never* forget! I picked him up as a trick. We went to my girlfriend's house, and we did our thing. And *all night* I was stuck with him. And we went out drinking, and he was buying me caps to fix, and we stayed in the Austin Hotel, and in the morning ... Like he had two days on shore leave, so in the morning he gave me 60 dollars to go score two more caps, and I come back, and we had breakfast in bed. We went downstairs and had a few drinks. We went out. I says, "I'm goin' workin'." He says, "No, you're not." I says, "Well, when I get sick, what an I gonna do?" "You know what you're gonna do," he says, "You'll just keep quiet!" So it was about an hour after we had our beer, I started to get sick. And I went out, he gave me the money and I bought four more caps and then I fixed'... I did that all night ... I was off work for *two days!* I just had a good time. Went out dancing all over the place! He tried to talk me out of fixin'. We went up and he met my aunt. And my aunt wanted to help me ... you know ... kick. And he suggested I stay with my aunt, so I did. She didn't do me any good, though. Her and her nagging! Bitching at me all the time!

#7   *THE JUNKIE AND THE COP* (by BUGSY)

Hey, I was fixin' two caps one night and they kicked the door. And I had the fit like this ... And I stuck it in my bra, not thinkin'. And the cop come over and says, "Undo your top." And I says, "Fuck you!" He says, "Undo your top!" I says, "No way!" He says, "Well, I'll do it!" I says, "Take your hand away!" So, while I'm undoing it, I'm pushing ... Like I figured ... I stuck the needle in my tit, so I was gonna skin it. And as I was pushing the needle in it, I felt it all running down, all over my stomach, and all over my nice blue pants ... and ... the sons of bitches! I pushed all the way down, and I took it off and says, "Here!" Yeah ... He was lookin' "Possession of heroin" *[clowning intonation]*. I had two more caps in my bra. Now, this cop takes me downtown and I got the handcuffs on me, like this. *[putting her hands behind her back]*. There's one on this side of me, and one on that side of me. And when this one here, in front of me, is writing, the other one over here is watching. And when he's writing, *this* one is watching me. And I'm sitting like this, all charm, trying to get in there and get those two caps outta there, because they were going to take me upstairs and skin me. So the cop says "Now," he says, "what are you gonna do?" I says, "Now, I'm gonna go out and make some more money so I can fix, hey?" So he says, "Well ... you have nothing else on you, hey?" I says, "Do you think I'd be *dumb* enough to be *sitting* here if I did?" So he says, "Well, we'll get you frisked anyways." So, he phones up and they had no matron up there to do the frisk. Phew! He says, "O.K. We'll give you this to appear in Court." I says, "O.K." He gave me this thing to appear in court, and I left.

I got out on the street and now I haven't got a fit and I have two caps. Well, right at Main and Hastings, there, on the side where the Cop Station is, right down on the edge, was a fit laying, in a package. Somebody had dropped the fit in a package. Well, I figured, "What the hell is going on? Somebody ... Maybe I'm hallucinating ..." Anyways, I picked it up, and I had an aspirin tube on me, and I dumped all the aspirins, and I went to the X Hotel and I fixed. And I just finished fixin', and I hear the cops out there! "Police! Open up." Everything went down the toilet! I'm glad I got it in my arm! He says, "What are you doin' in there?" I says, "Nothing!" He says, "How come you got ..." I didn't know, but I had black on my hand, and before they come, I went like this *[passing her hand over her forehead],* so I had fingerprints, like this all over my head! "What are you doing?" I says, "Nothing." He says, "How come you got black on your head?" "I <u>ain't</u> got black on my head!" And I looked in the mirror, and I says "Oh ... Well, I don't know ... Probably from something ..." Well, fuck!

(Note: The black came from the spoon in which she had been "cooking" the heroin and its significance could not be mistaken.)

#8   *SLASHING* (by BUGSY)
Most of the time, I was drunk when I slashed. Like once, I was out on a pass. I came back pissed, I couldn't even walk. I told the guard at the gate, "I'll walk down." He says, "I don't think you'll make it!" "Sure, I can make it!" (It wasn't on my pass that I couldn't drink They wanted to crime me, but they couldn't.)   Anyway, I never slashed in jail. I don't think you'd do it when you're sick, because when you're sick, you're really tender. You can't take any kind of pain. I did most of it when my daughter died.

One girl did it in here for no reason at all. One night, she broke a window and slashed her wrist on it. Everybody ignores them! That's what they're looking for *[sympathy].* There's S ... She's a bit upstairs, but she slashed one night. I looked at her and I says, "Are you proud of that?" She says, "No." I says, "Did you try to gain attention from it?"

She says, "I dunno ..." I says, "I think you did." I says, "Think about it for a minute." And she thought, and then she says, "Yeah ..." And then I says, "Did you get your attention?" She says, "No." I says, "Look at me. I'm ashamed of wearing a short-sleeved dress because of them." Then, I says, "Aren't you going to be ashamed of them when that thing heals?" I says, "It's not going to go away like you've never done it." I says, "You'll always have a scar there."

Me, I just blew my top. It was either slash or die, one of the two. I tried to jump off the bridge, but they wouldn't let me. The cops got me.

#9   *THE REMORSEFUL COP* (by BUGSY)
When I was working, there was this cop come to see me at work. And he says, "I got to talk to you." And I says, "Yeah, I know, I bet!" And he says, "I'll be up to you when you've finished." So he says, "I'm taking you home." I says, "I don't need a police escort home! I live two blocks away!" There was two blocks downhill ... "Well," he says, I've got to talk to you anyway!" "Well, talk now," I says, "this is my break anyways, so we can talk now." "No," he says.

So he came back to pick me up, and we went driving around and I was drinking all night at the restaurant. Before I left and I was waiting for him to come, I had two triple rye and cokes and four Southern Comforts, so I wasn't in too good shape! Well, he's driving and talking to me, and I'm falling asleep! When I woke up, we were up in Little Mountain. "Where am I?" He says, "You're up at Little Mountain." So I opened the door to get out and I says, "Wait! What the hell am I doing up here?" He says, "Well, I've been talking to you." I says, "I haven't heard a word you've been saying!" He says, "I know!"

Anyways, I walked around the park for a while, and he talked to me. And he says they're trying to bring in my charges from Calgary. So I says, "So, let'm do it!" I says, "It doesn't bother me anymore," I says, "I'm gonna get time anyway! One way or another .." Well, he says, "I'm trying to hold off." I says, "What for?" I says, "You fuckin' arrested me! You're my arresting officer and here you sit trying to tell me you're holding back other charges?" I says, "Until what? Until I finally get released from Oakalla and walk out the gate, and then you're going to pick me up? Forget it!" Anyways, I came in here *[jail]* and he's been to see me three times. And I told him I didn't want him out here then. Nothing to discuss!

I don't know ... He feels bad about busting me, 'cause I got thirteen months for soliciting, my first charge. And he feels bad about it. He saw me in court when the judge gave me the time, you know, and his jaw almost dropped down to his knees. And I says to him, "Thanks a lot!" And he says, "Wait a minute! I didn't know you were going to get that much time," he says, "I would have dropped the charges a long time ago!" I says, "Hey, you charge somebody, you don't turn around and drop them for nothing," I says, "Whatever plans you got up your sleeve, forget it!"

#10 *THE LITTLE OLD MAN* (by BUGSY)

I had this little ol' man, once ... And this was cute. He took me out. He paid me just for a straight, and his time was up, and he hadn't even got it hard. And he wasn't drunk, he had had nothing to drink. And he says, "Oh dear! he says, my time's up!" Like, it was him that kept the time, I wasn't even lookin'. "My time's up," he says, "and all I got is 20 dollars more!" So, I says, "Well, I'll tell you what," I says, "you give me another ten, just ten of it, I says, and you can stay for another twenty minutes." And he says, "Are you sure it'll be O.K.? Your boy friend's not gonna get mad?" I says, "I haven't got a boy friend." So he says, "I guess it'll be O.K., then." And he stayed. And he still couldn't get it up! So he says, "Well," he says, "are the banks closed yet?" And I says, "No." So he went to the bank, and he came back. I didn't think he would come back, I really didn't! And he was ... Before he left his face was just beet red, he was so embarrassed hey? And he says: "Well," he says, "I'll come back." And I says, "O.K., sure, sure!" You know, I was standing outside and I had my back ... I didn't know he was coming back ... I had my back turned. And he come up and he tapped me on the shoulder, and I turned back again. "This time," he says, "this time I've got 200 dollars, we can stay for a long time!" I just cracked up laughing! I was with him for about two hours. He made it four times! I got the 200 dollars, too. Plus the other 60! So, it wasn't too bad ...

#11 *NERVES OF STEEL* (by JULIE)

Now, I sat one time in a beer parlour with my husband. And we sat there drinking, near a complete tableful of students from B.C.I.T. And I just walked up and plucked up a purse. She was just talking, drinking, laughing. I went up to the parking lot, checked it out. I saw she had a bank account with quite a lot. So there I went, got the car keys (the bank was just up the block), pulled all her money out of her account. I decided to write a withdrawal, 'cause they don't have pictures on bank accounts, nowadays. So I went, pulled all her money out of her bank account, took what I wanted out of her purse, and returned the purse back with the cheque. She didn't notice at all! And I had all the money! And I finished my drink and then I went out.

#12 *THE MARK* (by JULIE)

Well, this one mark ... I was hitchhiking through the States. I tripped in old Las Vegas ... Hey, that place is just where it's at, as far as I'm concerned. You could never find such an all night city, and me at seventeen, that was where it was at, to see these bright lights, hey? Like you're young and you can play the game a lot better when you're young and fresh, you know? These older men figure, "Well, Jesus Christ! There, the old lady's at home, and I get me a young whippersnapper here." I can just see them taking it all in! You know ... They're there for a good time, that's plain to see, you know, without even asking. They're in that city for good times. So you're open season on their wants. There's your marks, right there! You pretty well get them to buy your entire wardrobe if you play your cards right. I mean ... That's just material things that they like to see you in, you know, if they're going to stick around ... It sometimes works to give the impression that you're not too enthused about things. Then, they'll go out and keep on buying and buying. And another good thing, you know, is to say you're out of jewellery and "Surprise me, honey!" And they'll go out and they'll buy you ... tiaras, you know, if you wore them! It's something else! Because they want to keep you happy ..

Photograph courtesy of Lincoln Clarkes

(Worldwide Green Eyes)

APPENDIX E

THE UNLUCKY LOGGER'S SONG

Alan Salo, a folklorist at the University of British Columbia in the 1970s, translated for me a BC Finnish song, probably dating from the 1920s and relating the misfortunes of a logger come to spend his money in Vancouver.

While wandering about on Hastings Street in the evening/There I met a pretty girl/ She winked her eye/With her hand closer to me she coaxed.

"Hey," whispers the girl, "dear you are to me/For a short time all your own /It will cost you a dollar: Not much, is it?"/A dollar I stick in her hand and step onto the street.

But the woman had a grave disease/ "cankers," which are quite dangerous/Hell's whore, when so young, she too, the French disease has/Well, it can't be guessed even if you examine each hair.

The next time for sure more care you will take/When you pay the medical bills/Your pockets become empty/It's chilly to always stand an hour to take a piss.

APPENDIX F

A MARK'S STORY.

I see a man in his forties hitch-hiking on the highway. I'm in no hurry and I stop. He looks nice but he smells of alcohol, which makes me somewhat suspicious. A conversation starts:

- Where are you'going?
- Not very far, down the road. I have to see a guy at the garage. I'll tell you where to stop.
- I'm going to X., to snowshoe. It's a beautiful day!
- Yes, but rather chilly.
- What sort of work do you do?
- I work at the docks, in one of the sheds. My job is to control the merchandise that is stocked there.
- What sort of merchandise?
- Everything, but mainly imports from Japan, you know, cameras, electronic equipment, televisions. That's why I'm going to the garage, to make arrangements for the delivery of a 24"colour T.V.... Hot merchandise... You know what I mean... I'm selling him a $700 T.V. for $250, brand new! I hope you're not a cop or a lawyer, or something?
- No, I'm just a teacher.
- If you're interested, I have a $400 Nikkon camera that you can have for $125.
- I don't really need a camera, but I can ask some of my friends. But I'm looking for a small black and white T.V. Do you have any?
- *(Slight hesitation)* No... No... But I can get some. How many do you need?
- One for myself... perhaps more... I have to ask some of my friends. What kind are they?
- Sanyo... 21"... Portable.
- Do you have anything smaller.., say 17" or 19" in Panasonic or Sony?

- No, but I'll see what I can get.
- How do you get the merchandise? I've heard about "hot merchandise" sold by port employees. Are there no controls?

His answer was vague. What I remember is that entire trucks were deviated to the wrong shed after custom control. Merchandise was then taken out item by item.

- I don't quite follow, but I suppose you have to work there to understand the intricacies of custom control and storage.
- Exactly! Anyway, I'm not supposed to reveal too many details of our operations! I don't know you... You could squeal to the cops!
- No, I'm not a cop.
- Are you interested in buying boxes of frozen filet mignon steaks? 50lb boxes?
- Frozen steaks?

- Yeah! The best filet mignon! Some people buy 200 pounds and fill their freezer right up!

- I don't have a freezer. Anyway, I'm kind of reluctant to buy meat on the sly. You never know...

- Nothing to worry about! It's government-inspected meat. I eat some every day.

It must be good meat because the man looks in top shape! I learned at the beginning of our conversation something I forgot to mention: If that man smells of alcohol, it's because he is Irish and he celebrated St Patrick's Day the day before.

- No, thank you. Where can I reach you about the T.V.? Do you want to give me a number where I can reach you?
- No, I can't give you my number, it's too dangerous! I don't know you.
- I told you that I don't have anything to do with the cops! I'm a teacher. I can show you some I.D.
- No need! No need! Give me you number and I'll call you.

I was a bit hesitant to give my name and number to a thief. Could he not take my address with the intention of burglarizing my apartment while I was at work? After some hesitation I finally gave him my home and office phone numbers. He jotted them down on a small piece of paper.

We had arrived at the garage. He told me to let him off, assuring me that he would call me in a few days. He needed some time to make the necessary arrangements. We said goodbye and I continued on my way.

Two days later, I received a phone call at the office. The man told me he had some T.V.s but they were bigger than what I had asked for. I said, "O.K. Save one for me." "Do you have any friends who would be interested?" he asked. I went to the office next door to ask a friend. He wanted one. We said that we would even take a third set for another person we knew who might need one. The price of each T.V. set would be $75. The man told me the exact place where we were supposed to meet him the next morning at 10 o'clock. He added again that he did not want to see any cops.

My friend and I discussed the matter and thought that the T.V. sets would be delivered to us in closed cardboard boxes. But, after all, the man could be trying to swindle us and he could have filled the boxes with charcoal or dirt... So, we decided to bring along a knife which could be used to open the boxes quickly.

The next day, we parked the car at the prescribed place, which was near the docks. After waiting for fifteen minutes, our man knocked at the side window to have the back door unlocked. He got in the car, sat down, and told us to hurry because it was not safe to stay there. He gave us immediately the directions to the shed where the transaction was supposed to take place. We parked near the fence restricting access to the docks. Then the man told us: "That'll be $225: " We turned around, very surprised. "But, we want to see the merchandise!" we said. "But, this is not what I told you," he answered. "I told you that I needed the money first, to give it to the guy in charge of the loaded truck!"

My friend then said that he was no longer interested. However, I did not want to give up so easily. I said to the man: "Well... I didn't understand that..." "Hurry up," said the man, "it's not safe for me to stay here too long!... Oh, God! It's hard to do business with you! Take it or leave it, the way it was agreed!" I replied: "We're sorry... but you must understand... you see, we don't know you... You might be a crook and leave with our money!"

The man then talked more calmly and agreed with us, but said that after having the money it would take him only five minutes to be back with the three T.V. sets: he only had to go to the truck and give the money to the driver. I then asked him to leave some piece of identification with us, but he did not have any wallet or I.D. He repeated that he could not stay all day with us! I then decided to risk the price of one T.V. set and gave him $75. He left immediately. We could not even tell which way he went because on the one hand it was wintertime and the car windows were fogged up, and on the other hand we felt ashamed to doubt the word of a man who could be honest, and we did not want to watch him too closely and show him that we did not fully trust him.

Silence prevailed in the car... But after fifteen minutes, my friend and I literally burst out laughing. We had understood that we had been had. We got out of the car. Our man had completely disappeared. We drove around, but in vain. Finally, we drove back to the college, our knife unused. It was obvious that we should have known better!

(Story collected anonymously in 1977)

ACKNOWLEDGEMENTS

I am most grateful to my academic advisor, Elvi Whittaker, who has since become a good friend of long standing. She guided me through this work with care and rigour. Her encouragements have been precious. In street parlance, she is "good people."

I am equally grateful to John for his infinite patience and continued support, which have endured well over half a century. My children, Peter, Stephen, Kim, Nicholas, and Alexa, have grown up seeing me endlessly absorbed in projects of one kind or another. Perhaps it was not always easy for them, and I thank them for their kindness.

I wish to thank the Canada Council for their financial support during the research and writing of my dissertation, as well as the staff of the Lower Mainland Regional Correctional Centre for their courteous assistance.

I'm grateful to Professor Belshaw for initiating the process of publication of this work and seeing it to its conclusion.

My thanks are due to Lincoln Clarkes *(Worldwide Green Eyes)* for allowing me graciously to use photographs from his *Heroines* series. I am equally thankful to a few kindhearted individuals, Nick Layton, Stephen Hansen, Kathryn and Hannah Sellam, for providing sorely needed technological instruction.

Last, but definitely not least, I owe a debt of gratitude to those women, tricksters yet mostly good souls, who shared a small part of their knowledge with me.

Vancouver 2010

<hr>

[i] In Canada the term East Indian is used because of the necessity to distinguish from indigenous Indians.

www.ingramcontent.com/pod-product-compliance
Lightning Source LLC
Chambersburg PA
CBHW020608270326
41927CB00005B/229